Achieve Your Apex

How to Maximize Your Strengths, Create Predictable Results, and Thrive in Every Facet of Your Life

Chad Hyams

Cover Design: Josiah Ubben, Hadyn Pistochini

www.AchieveYourApex.com

To Nita:
all ways and always

Contents

Gratitude

I have been told that this section is usually titled Acknowledgements. Well, this isn't the first time I'm choosing to do something my own way. Plus, I don't want to just acknowledge people, I want to express my gratitude to them. There are many people who have been part of this journey. Just by reading this section, you've become one of those people, too. Thank you for picking up this book.

Putting my thoughts into a book has been a goal of mine for some time. I'm excited to see it finally come to fruition and deeply grateful to all those who helped me get to this point.

First, of course, is Nita, my wife. I am so grateful you came into my world. It is your support, your belief, and the way you challenge and cheer for me that make me want to be a better person every day. Without you, writing this book would have remained an unreachable summit that I would still be staring up at.

Simone, my daughter, fills me with gratitude and makes me proud every day, as she grows, learns and starts the journey towards her own apex.

I am thankful for the group of guys who have been in my life since high school, and with whom I remain close today: Ern, Rob, Dave and Andrew. Included in that group is I.J., a wizard with the pen. Without his help, these pages would still be stuck in my head.

I am deeply appreciative to all of those who were kind and generous enough to share their personal stories with me. Some I included in the book and some I didn't, however all are equally meaningful.

Thank you to the many people I've had the pleasure of teaching, coaching and working with over the years, who helped me flesh out these ideas by acting as test subjects, even if they didn't know they were doing it at the time.

I am grateful to all of the teachers in my life, from those in school who challenged the way I thought and encouraged me to focus on my strengths to those in other parts of my life from whom I have learned lessons that are just as important.

To Clint – I stalked you into a friendship and you have since become a mentor in multiple areas of my life. Thank you for your wonderful support over the years and for co-writing the foreword with Ben.

To Ben – what can I say? Grateful isn't a big enough word. Your support, leadership and vision have continued to create opportunity in the world for so many people, including me. Thank you for your friendship, for co-writing the foreword with Clint, for letting me stay in your basement, and for the fact that meeting you helped lead me to Nita.

Thank you to Josiah and Hadyn Nicole for their expert design work on the cover. You captured the book's essence and tolerated my many questions, challenges and changes to arrive at something truly beautiful.

I am grateful to my dad. While he is no longer with us, many of the lessons he taught helped create the foundation for the ideas I offer. Even when I couldn't see it, Dad always had my back and supported me every day.

Lastly, the person who has encouraged me from the very beginning, and who has seen me through every step toward my personal apex, is my mom. Mom, you have always been there to cheer me on, and I am grateful for your unconditional love and never-ending support.

Foreword by Ben Kinney

I have climbed a lot of mountains in my life, literally and figuratively. I have reached the apex in many different areas, and I have also quit halfway up more mountains than I can remember.

The mountains in my life that I have yet to summit are the ones I think about the most, not the ones where I reached the top. The book you are about to read could be the secret ingredient missing from your life that can allow you to unlock your true potential.

I have known Chad for many years. I have seen him at the worst points of his life and at his peaks. What makes him rare is that he has been living at the summit for a long time in all areas of his life. Chad is a coach of coaches, a mentor, a teacher, and a humble and hard-working person.

Yet I don't want you to be impressed with Chad while reading this book, because that isn't the goal. The goal is for you to be empowered to take action in whatever areas of your life you need to change. The models and systems you will learn are simple, effective, and applicable to anyone. Let me expand on that for a moment.

I have spent years wondering how it is that results in life, careers, and business are so unevenly distributed across my peers when we all have the same amount of time, access to education, work in the same economy, and live in the same areas. After investing much time on this subject, I have concluded that it comes down to one simple thing. Those who implement models and systems live an extraordinary life, while those who don't live an unpredictable one.

Have you ever reflected back on the previous year and thought to yourself that you have wasted time, lost opportunities, ruined relationships (or stayed in the wrong ones), that you make decent money but always have money issues, and that, at the end of another year, no matter what you may have tried to change, the results are no different?

Please excuse the language for a second, but it's time to get a little pissed off. Change comes when we ourselves change.

Is this your year to change? Is this the last year you're willing to be broke? To be unhealthy or overweight? To have new ideas but take no action? To be busy all the time but not productive? To give all your time to work instead of to your family or loved ones?

If this is truly your time, then you are ready for the change that *Achieving your Apex* is going to provide. This is your time to summit. This is your time to reach new heights in your personal life, your career, your finances, your health, and your relationships.

Say it with me. "This is MY year. MY year to become the person my dreams require."

Sit back and get ready to learn, reflect, create, plan and execute. This is a take-action book written by a take-action person, filled with simple models that will help you reach your apex.

Ben Kinney

Foreword by Clint Swindall

We all want to be better. In many cases, we know what it takes. We need to plan better, communicate better, focus better, lead better, perform better, eat better, and connect better. Depending on what you are trying to achieve, you need to do better, and you know it.

If we know, for the most part, what we need to do to be better, why don't we experience and witness more success in this life? Perhaps we aren't willing to hold ourselves accountable. Perhaps we have become a part of the "good enough" crowd and are ready to accept a life of mediocrity. Or perhaps we have chosen not to take the necessary steps to get better.

The best thing about getting better at anything in this life is that it is not difficult. It does, however, require some work. It will demand a willingness to consistently apply proven fundamentals to our lives. In *Achieve Your Apex*, Chad Hyams shares some fundamentals that will make it simple and doable for anyone interested in being better.

As a professional speaker, I have the honor of meeting some incredible people worldwide. Chad was one of those people. From the moment I met him at a conference in Orlando, I could tell that his thirst for knowledge was matched only by his desire to help others. I have watched him serve others as a speaker, trainer, coach, and now, an author. In a world where many people seek to be served, a devotion to helping others is an honorable commitment.

I'm thankful for Chad and his message. As we navigate this life, we need a roadmap to become better. We need someone with a track record of success guiding others to achieve their apex. For years now, Chad has experienced success as a coach, helping people maximize their performance. He has done it by simplifying the process of bringing multiple areas of our life together to find the best version of ourselves. This book is our opportunity to see what he's been doing for years as a coach.

For those who have achieved great success, this book will provide reminders of some of the things you did along the way – perhaps some of the things you stopped doing as you developed new daily habits. A significant part of ongoing success is recognizing the mid-course corrections needed to maintain excellent performance.

For those on the road to great success, this book will provide some specific takeaways to guide you on your journey. Chad will make you think about your ordinary day differently and challenge you to examine how you maximize what you do well and manage what you don't.

This is more than a book on becoming the best version of yourself. This is a guide that will require your active participation. Get ready to highlight key points and make notes along the way. Once you're done, go back and reread it. And as you continue your upward move toward becoming a better you, share these principles with others so they, too, can reach their apex.

Have a pleasant journey up the mountain!

Clint Swindall

Introduction

My mom was a teacher. I believe watching her help others grow, learn and evolve planted a subconscious seed in me. In every professional incarnation I passed through, this showed up as both a tendency and a skill. I would always find myself in unofficial teaching or training situations that translated into helping others improve some aspect of themselves. When I started doing formal training through keynotes, workshops and large events, people seemed to respond strongly, and many of them began asking if I could make the time to speak with them one-on-one, effectively acting as a coach.

Helping others seemed to suit me better than anything I'd done before. It was the thing that felt the most honest and rewarding. People started reporting positive results to me. They strengthened relationships; they explored new areas of personal growth; they lost weight; they surpassed their personal bests in business. Others started coming forward to request my help. I was heartened by the mix of those who approached me, all with the same desire: to do better, and be better.

I left the role I was in and made this my full-time pursuit, developing an overall philosophy and practical tools and techniques to apply it. Rather than "life coach," I decided the term "maximization coach" felt more accurate. People are already living life – my goal was to help them do it as well as possible, by being their advisor, cheerleader and challenger.

Achieve Your Apex is a collection of the lessons and strategies I teach to help my clients focus their vision, harness their strengths and seize their potential. I like the apex concept because I find both versions of it equally relevant. There are the traits and behaviors we can learn from apex animals and apply them in our own lives to get the best and most out of ourselves. And there is the apex of a mountain, representing that summit we all wish to achieve in our lives.

You'll see throughout the book that I'm a fan of acronyms and frameworks – starting with one I call the Apex A's, containing the five key elements to keep in mind as you take the first steps and embark on the journey.

The Apex A's

Aim. You can't hit goals if you don't define them.
Arrange. Repeated success comes from consistent planning.
Attempt. You can't succeed if you don't make the attempt.
Accountability. No one does it alone.
Amend. Everything is a work in progress.

While the book is divided into twenty individual chapters (all of which, apart from the last, conclude with a relevant story generously provided specifically for this book), the topics are all interconnected. Many of the stories in a given chapter can apply to several others. You'll also notice some consistent themes. For example, real estate comes up regularly, because that's a world in which I spent a significant amount of time. Physical transformations are reported often as well, since I went through a significant one myself and came to understand all too well the connection between our internal and external selves, and that when you achieve a certain level of mastery inside, it manifests on the outside. You'll note several Canadian references, since I was raised north of the border. Finally, you'll hear people talk about applying apex principles in both their personal and professional lives. These are intertwined, after all; each area of our lives affects every other.

In the end, we're all seeking the best version of ourselves. It can be a complicated quest. I hope you find this book helpful, and I wish you the best as you pursue your own apex.

Chapter 1: Optimize Your Environment

As a human being, you both occupy your own space and move through other spaces. You enter and exit a variety of these environments every day, likely not thinking about them too much or how well you function within them.

What if I asked you to pause and assess how effective the match is between these two sides of your daily coin: you, and the environments which make up your day? Would you have an answer? A lot of what we do, we do automatically, without thinking much about it, mostly to feel we're getting things done. We pass from this environment to that, ticking off the boxes in our to-do list, exhaling at the end of the day, then pressing repeat. This doesn't promote change; it encourages us to stay the same.

How do you maximize your environments, and yourself within them? First, by recognizing what they are, what they look like, and what they represent within the context of your general goals. Next, by thinking about ways you can better adapt to those settings and make improvements to your own functioning within them. And finally, by taking control and putting in place the conditions for you to do, and be, your best.

Understanding Your Environments

Let me ask you a question: Do you know your environment? Don't answer too quickly. I'm not asking you to go around the room and name things. I'm asking you to tell me about all the places and spaces in which you work, live, play – the various settings and situations in which you live the different parts of your life.

Let's take the environment in which you work, for instance. Is it big or small? Open or cluttered? Private or shared? At home on your own, or in an office with others? What about your play environment? Is it a makeshift gym in your basement? A nearby hiking trail? The local basketball court? The backyard trampoline? How about your preferred place to relax? Is it a dedicated meditation corner of your bedroom? The couch in front of the TV? A downstairs reading nook?

Where do you find yourself socializing? The local coffee shop? The yoga studio? Your parents' favorite restaurant?

You get the idea. We pass through a series of environments every day, each one for the purpose of achieving specific goals – sleep, eat, work, drive, shop, play, relax, connect. The list is endless. It's fair to say that, on average, we're so busy managing day-to-day life that we don't stop to think much about these environments while we're in them. We wake up, shower, get dressed. If we have kids, we tend to their needs and get them where they're going. We continue on to our own place of work, or back to our home environment. We spend a number of hours being productive, aiming to succeed, striving to get ahead. We carve out some time to be active. We buy food, prepare it, eat it. (Some days we say the hell with preparing it, so we just buy it and eat it.)

The days tend to go by in blurs. How many of these environments do you pass through on an ordinary day? Take a minute to think about it.

After you've come up with the answer, let me ask you another question: In each of these environments, how effectively do you function? How easily are you able to fulfill the purpose of being in that space at that time? How much or how little does each of these environments contribute to your overall vision for that day? How close are you to your best self in the first setting you occupy in your day? The second? The fifth? The last?

Close your eyes. Imagine your first environment of a normal day. What does it look like? What's in it? Who are you in it? Happy? Frustrated? Relaxed? Rushed? Contented? Worried? Rested? Weary? How about the next environment you usually enter? What characterizes it? What purpose does it serve? How consistently, how easily and how efficiently does it satisfy that purpose for you? Why or why not? The next? The one after that? By the end of a regular day, how many environments have you occupied, in what ways, for what reasons – and how effectively have you accomplished your goals in each of them?

Taking time to think about these questions connects you more closely with the environments that make up your hours, your days, and your life. I'm willing to bet you usually pass through these spaces, one to the next, without really considering how effectively you function within them.

Adapting to Your Environments

Pausing to reflect on your environments can help determine how much, or how little, they allow you to be your best you. Once you have an idea of that, you can then think about how to adjust to the environments in which you live, work and play in ways that will allow you to achieve your apex.

I'll give you a simple example. My mother, god bless her, was a typical mother – meaning she was always feeding me and my friends. The food Mom provided was comforting, though one wouldn't quite call it kale-based. Add to that the modern North American diet featuring lots of snacks and junk foods, and I wasn't exactly set up for success. Candy bowls were out constantly, and no sooner emptied by hungry teenage mouths than filled again. This was, to say the least, not a good environment for optimal physical health. The emotional environment Mom created was very positive and full of love, and feeding us constantly was one of the ways of expressing that love.

I wasn't able to reflect on this particular environment until years later. Once I was encouraged to think about it, I realized it – among other factors – was part of what led me, by my mid-thirties, to end up in the worst shape I'd ever found myself in.

In my home today, you won't see candy bowls. Pictures of my mom and reminders of her love and devotion, yes. However, my wife Nita and I have a mutual pact to keep the environment free of things that will make us physically unhealthy or tempt us to make poor choices. Part of achieving your apex is filling your space with things that provide positive energy, encourage healthy choices, and enable productive outcomes, while at the same time minimizing or, where possible, eliminating things likely to discourage or derail progress, productivity and positive choices.

You can't always choose the type of environment you're in, or the surroundings in which you find yourself. What you can choose is how you modify specific components of it to create a higher likelihood of good results.

It's rare that one of your given environments is all positive or all negative. Those we move through day to day are multifaceted. Consider again the example above regarding my mom and her penchant for constantly feeding me. As I said, though all the other parts of my home environment were positive, this one contributed negatively to my overall state, since food is, of course, a pervasive component of every day.

Millions of years of history reinforces that it isn't the environment that tells the tale; it's the way we adapt to it. Great white sharks, for example, have a special adaptation that allows them to live in water too cold for other predatory sharks. This distinct feature is called regional endothermy. Because of it, great whites have the unique ability to store heat generated by their muscles while swimming, which their circulatory systems then move to colder parts of their body. The result is that they have a warmer body temperature than the waters in which they swim. Even if they didn't choose their environment, they sure developed a perfect adaptation to allow them to thrive within it.

Great white sharks aren't the only apex predators that have developed special adaptations to flourish in their natural environments. Have you ever heard the rumor that crocodiles sleep with one eye open? It's true. And not just crocs – orcas do it, too. It's a phenomenon called unihemisperhic sleep, which involves the ability to shut down only one half of their brains while keeping the other half awake so that they can detect dangers lurking nearby. Like great whites, crocs and orcas didn't get the chance to cast a vote about the environments in which nature placed them. Instead, over eons, they've adapted to those environments in remarkable ways, allowing them to reach the highest level of functioning and maintain their place at the top.

Optimizing Your Environments

Taking time to reflect on the different environments through which you move is one part of achieving your apex. Thinking about the ways in which you can make personal adaptations to these existing environments is another. The third prong is determining how you can proactively design your own environments to enable success.

Optimizing your environments means making them conducive to the goals you want to achieve – physical, mental, emotional, and practical. Simple as it sounds, if you consciously put in place the conditions for success, success becomes easier to achieve. Seize control of your environments. Set them up in a way that success becomes the most likely outcome. When you put the right things in the right place for the right purpose, productivity and success will be natural by-products.

The optimal environment doesn't look the same for everyone. For you, an ideal physical workspace may include a perfectly organized desk above which hangs a single motivational image with a matching proverb; for me, it might be a messy desk covered with papers, and walls adorned with vintage movie posters. For you, peak mental state may involve meditating on a beanbag chair in the lotus pose; for me, it might be running three miles while listening to an inspiring playlist. For you, the model social environment might be a restaurant patio on Saturday night with lots of friends, drinks and conversation; for me, it might be snuggling on the couch with my wife watching a rom-com. What matters most is taking the time to think about what defines optimized environments for *you*, then doing all you can to create them. Control your environments so they don't control you.

Remember also that, just as you exert influence over your environment, your environment exerts influence over you – and the most powerful aspects of that influence are the other people in it. Who occupies the spaces you move through day to day? How do those people influence you and affect the decisions you make, the behaviors you choose? I told you one story about my mom; let me tell you one about my dad. In tenth grade, I came close to flunking several of my classes. My dad approached me one day and told me, in no uncertain terms, that I had a choice to make: I could be grounded for all of grade eleven, in which I would essentially do nothing apart from schoolwork, or I could find a new group of friends, since the ones occupying my current circle weren't too interested in things like getting good grades, respecting authority, or planning for a successful future. I chose the second of the options Dad had offered, deliberately spending more time with a different group of guys whom I knew a little, and getting to know their parents and siblings as well.

Dad had it right. Of the new group I surrounded myself with, one has become a successful lawyer, one has a leading role with Toronto's tourism association, one is an accomplished actor, one is a respected leader in sales, and one is a bestselling writer (who, I'm proud to say, helped me with this book). I'm grateful to my mom for creating an environment of love and warmth and my dad for forcing me to improve the friendships that would have a ripple effect on the rest of my life. My new friends celebrated my capabilities while keeping me humble and grounded. They helped me grow and evolve. They challenged me to take risks. And they remain among my closest friends today.

Take some time to evaluate your daily environments. Think about how many there are, what they represent in your daily life, and the goals you seek to achieve within each one. Consider what adaptations you can make to improve your functioning within them. Finally, design your spaces proactively and embed the conditions for success. In doing so, you will create the opportunities for you to be your best self, realize your goals, and achieve your apex.

Annette's Story

At one point earlier in my career, while I was living in Washington State, I entered into a relationship with a guy who worked in the same office as I did. For the first couple of years, things were great. Then they deteriorated quickly. The environment at home became just terrible. I was subjected to constant mental and verbal abuse. He put me down every chance he could, which deepened my already significant self-doubt. The toxicity of the atmosphere started to affect every other part of my life, too. My work started to suffer, my confidence went in the toilet, I stopped talking to family and friends, and I gained seventy-five pounds. I fell into a pattern where I'd go to the office, do my work, come home, and then find the quickest way to numb myself. Anything not to experience that poisonous environment.

There was this one moment, when I was on the ground, totally out of it, unable even to get up off the floor. My boyfriend stepped over me and told me to get a life. In that instant, for reasons I can't really explain, something inside me shifted. Though I knew I couldn't necessarily change my circumstances overnight, a voice inside told me I could take control of certain things, starting with my internal environment. It was the proverbial rock-bottom moment in which a switch went on and I felt my mindset do a hard, and necessary, gear-shift.

In both a good and bad way, I had experience doing this, because when I was a kid, I had to. My dad was a functioning alcoholic, who did all the things alcoholics do, in the loud and terrible way they do them. At that age, instead of listening to the yelling and drunkenness, I'd go to my room and create my own environment. It allowed me not only to survive, but to thrive. I did well in school, I played sports, I had friendships. I had created what I guess one would call a workable, or even positive, internal environment to combat the externally negative one.

Now, as an adult, I realized I was going through this experience a second time. In that instant when my boyfriend had told me to get a life, I didn't react the way I normally would have, which would have been anger or some other, similar, knee-jerk response. Because I couldn't get any lower, because I hated myself, because everything in my life was suffering, because I was self-medicating, it was as though, in that moment, all the usual types of responses went away and this cocoon grew around me. I don't know why. Maybe I'd been pushed too far and suddenly a little kernel of strength appeared. That's all you need to start making changes.

That little bit of strength allowed me to start taking baby steps forward. I joined a gym. I looked into networking groups. I hired a life coach. Even if I wasn't yet strong enough to leave the relationship, the combined effect of these personal steps I was taking had a positive overall effect that helped shield me from his bad treatment of me. I was able to focus on myself in a healthier way and develop more confidence in myself. I was allowed to start liking myself again, a little at a time. As a result, his abuse didn't affect me the same way it had, and it didn't trigger in me the same dangerous behaviors or vicious cycle as before. I felt resistant to it, because I'd started to build up my own strength from the inside.

What was interesting, and even more disturbing, was that my boyfriend started to behave even worse toward me in reaction to my newfound strength and self-assurance. I suppose he saw my attempt to create a more positive environment as an odd kind of threat, the way I guess all abusers irrationally interpret any sign of strength or resilience as something they need to quash by stepping up the combination of abuse, intimidation and humiliation. The more he saw me building myself back up, the more he tried to break me down.

Ultimately, I found the strength to leave him. Anyone who has been in an abusive relationship knows how hard this is, despite the fact that it looks easy or obvious from the outside. The other person gets you so down on yourself that you don't feel you have the strength to leave, or the resources, or even the right. You feel you aren't worthwhile. It wasn't until I created my own environment that I found the strength to leave. (As a side note that won't surprise anyone reading this, I later discovered that he'd been leading a double life in Vegas, supporting an escort there.)

The key was this: When I say I created my own environment, I mean both external and internal. Finding even that tiny bit of internal strength allowed me to start changing things in a practical sense, too. Making the mental connection to my own sense of courage, independence and self-worth was what allowed me to start doing things like eating better, exercising, and being more productive at work. I've improved my professional results, I've lost the seventy-five pounds. Most important of all, I know what I'm capable of, and that I answer to me.

In a way, I started to do these things on auto-pilot. At that point, I couldn't have said I was aiming for some specifically defined goal or well-defined picture of happiness. I just knew things had to change.

It was largely a solitary effort at first. I was slowly emerging out of that terrible cocoon, and doing so warily. Even when I started with my coach, I was pretty resistant. In our first meeting, he recognized that I was going through some pretty bad stuff, and he told me some very direct things that I didn't want to hear. Or rather, wasn't ready to hear. I had an aversive reaction to that because everything he was saying was resonating with me in a triggering way. I was still in protective mode. Wasn't ready to let anyone in. So it wasn't a linear path. There was plenty of two-steps-forward-one-step-back. Eventually I felt whole and free enough to let him, and others, in. I was ready to open up, let myself be vulnerable, and allow someone else to help me in my journey back to me. He helped me confront the hardest questions – the simple ones that make you take responsibility for your life. What do you need to do every day to start putting the puzzle back together? What are the parts of your environment you're going to change, and how? What kind of workout are you going to do tomorrow, and when? Each one of these is a piece of the puzzle. When you're managing all the pieces in a complementary way, the picture is whole, and it looks, and feels, that way. When you aren't, it's obvious that things are missing.

I now appreciate all too well how intertwined the mental and physical aspects of health are, and I continue to nurture both parts every day to be my best self, to continue forward in a way that's positive and productive, and to be accountable to myself every day.

Chapter 2: Maximize Your Strengths

In Chapter One, we talked about the importance of understanding your environment, adapting to the parts of it beyond your control, and optimizing it by creating the conditions for success. Taking these steps helps you establish a setting better suited to your goals and an environment more tailored to your strengths. Let's discuss the next part of achieving your apex: maximizing those strengths while leveraging your weaknesses.

Wait a minute, I hear you saying. *Leveraging my weaknesses? Don't you mean improving my weaknesses? Fixing them? Turning them into strengths?*

No, I don't.

The Abilities Spectrum

There's an exercise I do with my clients, which I'd like you to do now. Take a blank page. On the left side, list what you feel are three of your strengths. On the right, three of your weaknesses. Now I'd like you to give these six traits a rating, each from 1-10, 1 being the lowest, 10 the highest.

Now here's a question: Did you give a rating of no lower than 8 to each of the strengths? And a rating of no higher than 3 to each of the weaknesses? If not, please list other traits. If you rated one of your abilities above 3 or below 8, they are not, in my view, strengths or weaknesses. They are average, and therefore of less consequence.

Here's why. Those who perform at their highest potential know their true strengths and maximize them, while recognizing their weaknesses and minimizing them. Minimizing your weaknesses means managing them, and managing them means not letting them get in the way of maximizing your strengths. Sound circular? It should.

Research by the renowned author John C. Maxwell shows that, on a typical 1-10 scale, it is rare for the average person to be able to improve by more than three points on any particular trait. Furthermore, because your strengths are already high, it's worth doing the work to nudge them even higher, making those traits even more potent, and therefore bigger contributors to your potential success. If you're 9 on a certain strength, it's worth the effort to improve that one level higher because it's likely something that can help you stand out from the crowd, make stronger impressions, and accomplish bigger and better things.

On the other hand, if you decide you want to dedicate time to improving on one of your weaknesses, say something you rated a 2, while I admire you for wanting to, I also discourage it, because, after all that work, if you've improved that attribute by even two points, you've brought it up to a 4 – from low to low-average. How much of an impact will this change have on your potential success? I suggest not much.

I realize this may be coming off as cynical and that you may feel I'm saying it's impossible for humans to overcome their weaknesses. I'm not. What I'm saying is none of us is good at everything, we all have our inherent strengths and natural weaknesses, and we should play up those strengths as much as possible while doing enough active management of our weaknesses to prevent them from acting as barriers.

Let me share a personal example. I was never too organized as a child or a teen, and I'm still not very organized as an adult. I did learn fairly early, however, that I was good at talking to people, encouraging them, prompting them to action, and breaking down complicated tasks into simple steps. Others seemed to like to listen to me, and I seemed to have a talent for helping people get things done and achieve results. Maybe it's because I'm loud. Whatever the reason, I discovered this in a pretty clear way, the way one gets signals over time about what they're good at – and not so good at.

As I began my career and began to grow as a coach and speaker, I nurtured this trait as much as I could, practicing as much as possible, getting feedback from everyone who would offer it, and pushing myself into different situations to test and challenge myself.

At the same time, I managed my natural lack of organization by getting help from others, using technology, and planning ahead. I say "managed" to reinforce Maxwell's point. It isn't fair to say I truly got better at it, and it would be a total lie to say I turned it into a strength. I just put in enough measures and controls so that it wouldn't serve as a derailer and prevent me from using my strength to full advantage. I spent as much time as possible cultivating and maximizing my strength while spending just enough time managing a weakness that could have otherwise gotten in the way.

21

Let's go back to my writer friend I mentioned in the previous chapter. When we were teenagers, two things were clear to all those close to him: he could really write, and he had a really terrible sense of direction. (He won't mind my teasing him about it here. He teases himself about it as much as we do.) In adolescence and into early adulthood, he spent every spare hour honing this talent, writing in every form about every topic and getting feedback by submitting to publishers everywhere he could. He also got lost frequently, often in highly entertaining ways. (It was entertaining to us, at least.)

As he moved into adulthood and made writing his profession, he knew he had to get better at knowing where he was going out of practical necessity. When you're driving your friends to the movies and you take a wrong turn, it's something to laugh about; when you're going for a job interview or picking up your child from school, being a half-hour late because you couldn't find your way isn't so funny. In the same way I had to manage my poor organizational skills, he had to manage his poor directional sense, and using the same tools: getting help from others, using technology, and planning ahead.

Would my friend say his directional instincts are better today than they were in high school? Not in a million years. He'll be the first one to tell you that if he's driving somewhere on his own without a deadline or immediate responsibilities, the chances of him taking a wrong turn are just as high now as they were then. On the other hand, you can bet he'll never be late picking up one of his kids. He's leaned into his natural strength and maximized it for success, while at the same taking sufficient steps to keep that weakness in check, and prevent it from being an undue problem.

So: yes, there are some weaknesses you need to pay attention to, because they affect the general functioning of your daily life, and others in it. If your spouse says you need to communicate more openly, that's something you should work on, because it has implications for your relationship. If your boss gives you tips for being a more effective presenter, listen well, because it has consequences for your career. If you aren't a natural handyman and you need to replace your toilet, leverage the task to a professional, since doing it wrong could have serious ramifications for your home (and your pocketbook).

Your other weaknesses, however, merit less attention if they don't impact your daily functioning or get in the way of maximizing your strengths. Bringing your 2's to 3's and your 3's to 4's will have small effects on your life and little impact on your ability to make the most of your potential. That possibility lies in making the most of your strengths. It's much more likely for you to get even better at the things you're already good at than for you to transform your natural weaknesses and turn them into strengths. Traits that fall into the average range – all those 4's to 7's – well, I believe you ought not to fret too much about those, since they won't likely have a meaningful impact at either end. In other words, if you're an average piano player, skier, chef, juggler or woodworker, great – enjoy those activities as complements to the strengths that you seek to maximize and the weaknesses you seek to manage, and at the same time, don't worry about the need to move them up the scale. Achieving your apex doesn't include becoming average in as many ways as possible.

Tigers and Their Stripes

We often refer to our weaknesses as though we should be embarrassed about having them. Guess what? We all have them! Don't think of your abilities as things you do or don't have. All our different attributes lie along a spectrum, some at the high end, some at the low end, some nearer the middle. It's a wonderful thing that we all bring a unique mix of capabilities and competencies to life. It would be pretty boring if we were all the same – and very little would get done, imagined, or invented. Your combination of strengths and weaknesses is yours alone, shared by no one else in the world. Isn't that cool? I think it is.

Did you know that tigers have stripes both on their fur and on their skin? Similar to human fingerprints, this individual pattern distinguishes every tiger from every other. If you were to shave a tiger (though I don't suggest it), its pattern of stripes would still be visible.

Though we think of tigers in ways that lumps them all together, each member of the species is, just like ours, distinct. And while, when we think of tigers, we think of their magnificent appearance, their incredible strength and quickness, their overall mystique, we don't think about the fact that they, too, have "weaknesses." They are unnerved by loud sounds. They're spooked by fire. They have relatively low endurance compared to other apex animals. They can't climb trees. They are solitary animals, so if a tiger gets injured in a fight, it can die from starvation if not able to recover in time to hunt again.

Tigers maintain their apex position by making the most of their strengths. They hunt their prey strategically, pounce quickly, conserve energy. They stay patient. They make the most of their kills. By leveraging its strengths to such powerful advantage, this splendid animal sits at the top of its environment. Like a tiger, you have your own combination of abilities, your own goals, your own way of doing things, and your own strengths to maximize. You, with your own distinct stripes, are uniquely you. Your attributes and abilities are like the knobs or dials on a music sound board. The ideal positions of those dials will look different for you than for everyone else. What's more, at different times and in different situations, it makes sense for you to turn certain dials up and others down in order to leverage the strengths required of a given moment or circumstance while managing the weaknesses that could get in the way. The more regularly you can optimize that balance, the more often you will perform at your apex.

The Strength Zone and the OK Plateau

We work at things to see results, and are often told by experts that the work we do and the results we see represents the proverbial iceberg image: most of the work is invisible below the surface, as opposed to the small part we see above the surface.

How often have you heard fitness trainers tell you it's the last few reps of a set that lead to real results? Those last couple that you squeeze out when you've almost had it – those are the reps that are truly responsible for growing muscles and burning fat.

What about the target heart rate zone? No doubt you've heard that plenty of times, too: it's once we get our heart pumping fast enough and keep it in that zone that we start to really drive results. Everything before is getting into that zone; everything after is coming down from it.

Take that heart rate zone and think of it in terms of using those strengths of yours as often as possible – being in the strength zone. When you're deploying your 8-and-above abilities, you're performing in that zone. When using your average abilities, you aren't likely moving the needle in any significant way. When actively managing your weaknesses, you're doing preventive work. The more you can amplify your strengths and the more opportunities you can find to use them, the longer you're spending in the strength zone, and the more profound results you'll see. How much time should you spend in your strength zone? As much as possible. Because the more you do, the more productive you'll be, the more you'll accomplish, and the higher percentage of time you will spend in pursuit of your apex.

Moonwalking With Einstein author Joshua Foer uses a term called the "OK Plateau" to describe a kind of unconscious complacency, in which we become competent at a certain skill and then don't put any further effort into it because it's reached the point of "good enough." One example he uses is the ability to drive. Most of us, he suggests, learn to drive when we're teenagers, have a brief period of rapid improvement, and then stop bothering to get any better.

Let's put this in the context of the strength zone. I don't believe you need to become great at driving unless you're aiming to become a professional – or you find yourself getting in accidents all the time, in which case this is one of those weaknesses that impacts your daily life as well as those around you (in this case, in a very dangerous way). That goes for many of our abilities, since, as I said, most of them probably fall within the average range. There are two reasons to want to improve a trait: one is to turn it into a strength, and one is out of pure interest in self-improvement, commendable in itself.

OK-ness, says Foer, is the enemy of greatness. *Good To Great* author Jim Collins says, almost in parallel, "Good is the enemy of great." Many other leadership and performance experts offer similar phrases. I believe that, depending on what your strengths are and what you're aiming to achieve, good is just fine for many of your abilities. "Good" can mean a lot of those traits that fall between the 4's and 7's, which, as noted, don't tend to affect your potential to succeed either by sparking it or limiting it.

To return to one of the earlier examples, if you're an average pianist and you want to get better, by all means have at it, however, there's nothing wrong with being a "good" piano player, which the majority of people who have studied some piano in the world are. Again, unless you're intending to become a concert pianist or play in a professional ensemble, "good" is, as far as I'm concerned, just great. (This could also be because I have no musical talent whatsoever.)

The plateau is negative when it involves a strength you aren't maximizing. This isn't unusual, because when we're good at something, we're often not motivated to get better at it, for several reasons. People compliment us on it regularly. It already feels good when we do it. We're kind of impressed with ourselves that we can do it better than most others, so it doesn't naturally occur to us to improve it even more. It's here where I think the plateau is relevant –where a true strength of yours becomes, to your perception, okay, therefore you don't do the work to make the most of it. When it comes to your strengths, seek to identify what they are, where you can use them, and how you can make them as powerful as they can be. By not doing so, you're depriving the world (if not the whole world, then at least your immediate world) of something special.

Mat's Story

I was born in Poland and came to the U.S. at age three, when my family emigrated. We ended up first in New Jersey, then just outside of Pittsburgh. Eventually, I came to Kansas City to attend graduate school, and started to put down roots.

I worked professionally in the theater community for several years. Once I had a growing family and was seeking a way to make money and provide, I became intrigued by the HGTV flipping craze. I read books like *Rich Dad, Poor Dad.* Started going to local investor meetings. Since I wasn't in a financial position to buy anything myself, I decided the next-best choice would be to get my real estate license.

However, when I first got into real estate, I struggled. I would see others around me succeeding and I'd ask myself, *What are they doing?* Or more accurately, *What am I not doing?* I'd ask lots of questions of people and emulate their patterns and behaviors to correct my issues. I was driven to grow and succeed personally, and most of all to provide for my family. I wanted to take action. I wanted to really go after my goals. The drive was there; the results weren't. My positive intention wasn't enough. Something was missing.

Then I discovered something interesting. When I was able to get in front of people – which at first wasn't very often – they seemed to respond to me. If I could just manage to get to the point of a live conversation, my success rate increased dramatically. I'd discovered my natural superpower.

I was encouraged by colleagues and mentors to maximize this strength to every extent possible. They told me that the reason for my success in live interactions was that I wasn't fake or superficial – that I was bringing my real self into the room, and that people understood and responded to this authenticity. To me, it was just being my normal self. Others told me this ability to connect with people in a sincere way was something distinctive.

I developed a saying: "You can't build rapport till you get through the door." Meaning I knew if someone were to meet me in person, they would feel the real me, as opposed to just an unfamiliar voice on the phone. They'd be able to see that I come from a place of true mutual contribution. When you're in sales, the biggest initial hurdle is breaking down the stereotype that you just want to close as fast as possible and then move on.

Having discovered my superpower, I did everything possible to get in front of people, including developing scripts and strategies to help me secure appointments. It started to work more and more. I found that people indeed responded well when I had the opportunity to show my genuine self. Over time, I learned that I could take the basic learnings we were given as agents and put my personal stamp on it. The more I made it my own and the more people I got in front of, the faster my results grew.

I also started to realize that, though one wouldn't have thought a Masters of Fine Arts in Acting and Directing with an emphasis in Classical Theater and Stage Combat would contribute to a career in real estate, it actually did. After all, my job was based on scripts. That certainly appealed to me, and it came naturally. I was able to internalize the dialogue rapidly, take those words, and make them my own. Moreover, I found that the performative aspect of the job was likewise a natural fit. I started to get the chance to present to large groups, and found that I thrived. It had all the same aspects necessary to a good acting performance: tapping into people's emotions, taking them on a journey, using humor and conflict.

Most important of all, I brought the skill of listening to every interaction. My theater studies taught me to listen first. In acting, once you've mastered the script, the words, you have to listen to the person opposite you and be fully present so that you can respond effectively. I know now that agents who struggle tend to be constantly in "telling" mode, as opposed to listening to what's important to the person across the table and therefore understanding their true goals and motivations.

Now, a number of years later, having progressed in my career, I'm able to leverage my key strength by traveling around the country helping others find and make the most of their own superpower. And in my home office, I have a team of seven who possess lots of skills that I don't. I focus on the things I do well and delegate the rest to those with better-matched skills and instincts. In this way, we all row in the same direction toward the same ultimate purpose and create outcomes greater than the sum of the individual parts. And we always remind and encourage one another to discover, explore, nurture and maximize our respective strengths and superpowers.

Chapter 3: Define Your Goals

In the next chapter, we'll talk about making plans to achieve goals. In this one, let's discuss the goals themselves – and the importance of defining them first.

You can't, after all, hit a target that doesn't exist. I know, this kind of statement falls squarely within the category of *That's not news, Chad.* And you're right. It isn't exactly a radical thought. We aren't here to debate whether defining goals makes them easier to meet. That idea is so obvious, no one in their right mind would reasonably argue it.

However, in our desire to achieve and our instinct to accomplish, we often bypass even the most logical steps toward doing so. It's one of those strange occupational hazards of being human. I'm sure you can point out numerous examples of head-scratching behaviors, both those you've seen and those you've done. Not going to the doctor when you know you're sick; eating food you know is terrible for you; ignoring the person you're attracted to in a bizarre attempt to make them like you. So much of what we do flies in the face of all reason, yet we do it. I don't know what percentage of the time on average we do the behavior that makes the most sense in a given moment, though I do know that, at least in my own case, it's far below one hundred.

So, yes, we kick logic to the curb more often than we'd like to admit, conceding instead to the power of primitive impulses, immediate gratification, or, sometimes, just that oddly compelling itch to simply do the less sensible thing, because…well, who knows why? (Message me directly if you have the answer – I'd love to know!)

In the case of hitting goals, we frequently skip the first and most important stage, pinning down the goal, because we want to get to the more fun, meatier stuff: pursuit, implementation, execution – getting to the prize at the end. The doing instead of the talking. The practical rather than the theoretical. The part that feels like progress over the part that feels like planning.

You can see it all the time in various contexts. A common example is the business meeting at the end of which two colleagues walk out and one says to the other, "Do you get what we're supposed to do? I have to say I wasn't totally clear on the objective." Typically, what happened was this: ideas were shared, responsibilities discussed, and an elaborate critical path or beautiful flow chart was presented with lots of arrows, triangles, colors and starbursts, however, because of the collective enthusiasm for diving into action, no one noticed that the most crucial question wasn't asked: What specifically are we aiming to get done?

The Power of Defining

When you name a goal and place it within explicit boundaries, you immediately accomplish a number of other things to help increase your odds of success. Is defining your goals essential to succeeding, or just helpful?

To answer that question, let me ask you a different one: How many times have you accomplished something great through random action? When we do random things, we get unpredictable results – which can be fun, humorous, exciting and memorable. This book, however, isn't about the time you and your friends spontaneously hopped in the car and drove a hundred miles to that burger joint in the next state (although that does sound wonderful – and delicious). We're talking about what you need to do to achieve your goals. The first vital step is defining them. Here are half a dozen reasons why.

⌃ **It unifies.** Stating an objective in a vivid and unequivocal way immediately provides everyone with a common purpose. The variety of metaphors you hear in the course of a typical business day to describe this – *singing from the same hymn sheet, rowing in the same direction, speaking the same language* – are all accurate. You know if the opposite situation is afoot, because that's when you hear the other types of expressions, like *The left hand doesn't know what the right hand is doing*, meaning a clear goal hasn't been defined or communicated, so even though people may be working hard, they don't know what they're working towards.

This applies equally to personal, individual goals. Saying to your friends "I think I might be into journalism" doesn't give them much of an opportunity for specific encouragement. However, saying "My goal is to be lead anchor of the top regional news station within ten years" tells them exactly what you're aiming for, implies a plan for getting there, and automatically elicits both shared interest in the goal as well as the ability to provide help where possible. Everyone who knows about this very precise objective can lend support by echoing it back to you, celebrating milestones along the way, and helping you stay confident, motivated, focused and energized. You're setting a specific target for yourself and at the same time helping others be helpful to you, because it's a lot easier, more effective, and more inspiring, for your best friend or colleague or mom or the local barista to say, "Can't wait to see you on the anchor desk!" than it is for them to say, "Good luck with journalism."

⅄ **It keeps you on course.** And, when necessary, it allows you to right the ship. Think of a compass, which allows us to maintain course toward an intended destination by constantly recalibrating direction even amid potentially disorienting forces. Because the compass's needle always points toward magnetic north, all that's necessary to stay on track is a simple measurement of the angle between the desired destination and the magnetized needle.

Taking just one measurement at the beginning of the voyage isn't sufficient, though; by the end of it, you could be miles off track. By re-adjusting at regular intervals, you make sure to navigate toward the goal with as little deviation as possible. On any journey, it's necessary to keep checking where you are on the path and reminding yourself where the destination lies. Using this metaphorical compass, if your goal is the fixed point on the horizon, even if you pause, veer off, or camp for the night, it's still there, and the regular measurements ensure you never stray far from your bearing. You've heard people use the business phrase "It's a moving target." What they mean is that the destination keeps shifting because no compass is being used.

⅄ **It places edges around the vision.** It's hard to connect with, latch onto or rally around intangibles. Those who say "I want to lose weight" are usually less successful than those who target a specific number of pounds to lose by a precise date. The first statement provides only the vaguest sense of what you're aiming for; the

31

second immediately defines two beneficial constraints: the specific target, and the precise time frame in which to meet it. No matter the size or scope of your aim, the more defined your parameters, the simpler you make it on yourself to succeed.

Imagine you're a painter. Whether you're painting a flower, a full garden or an entire landscape, your first decision is what's going to be in the frame. Only after you've made this decision are you then freed to make all the other relevant ones – the kind of canvas you'll use, the type of paints, the size and dimensions, the perspective. That first decision about where the boundaries are enables you to develop the picture from start to finish with no accidental change in focus. While you can change styles, apply different techniques, and even start all over if you want, what's meant to be within the frame remains.

The real-time version of this is represented every time you snap a photo. You position the lens, frame whatever you're shooting, zoom in or out, land somewhere between tight focus and full panorama, then, once you're happy with the boundaries, you tackle the other details – holding the camera at the right eye level, ensuring proper lighting settings, somehow getting your kids to smile at the same time instead of doing bunny ears on each other. You come away with your result by having first defined what belongs within the edges.

▲ **It creates excitement.** No doubt you've experienced examples of the reactions people have to goals both well and poorly defined. At a conference, when the president of the company says, "We're going to be great next year," it's met mostly with mild responses and hushed side conversations about what exactly this means. On the other hand, if you hear, "Our goal for next year is to get sixteen percent market share," or "We want to be the top brand in the country within three years," or "We are going to divest ourselves of our lowest-performing products over the next four quarters because we've done a detailed analysis projecting that if we shift one third of our resources to our top five bestselling

32

items, we should realize a twelve-percent increase in revenues," much different types of responses are likely. Outlining the specific goal immediately creates the possibility of its being met and puts it within your sphere of influence.

- ⌃ **It reduces anxiety.** A clearly defined goal doesn't just create focus, it also produces ease and a sense of security. When you can repeat a statement that tells you exactly what you're aiming for – not why you're aiming for it, or how you're going to achieve it, rather *what it is* – it grounds your perspective and provides a rudder to your energy. When teaching a child to ride a bike, it's always easier when you say, "See if you can stay on for five seconds" or perhaps, the next time out, "See if you can make it to the end of the street once" then, maybe, "See if you can sing all of Happy Birthday while riding." This has nothing to do with how to ride a bike. It's strictly a matter of framing clear goals – small at first, then increasing – in the simplest way possible.

- ⌃ **It creates the thing to work backwards from (and toward).** To repeat what I said at the beginning of the chapter, what should be obvious to any of us is that you can't hit a target if you don't know what it is. Consider a game of darts. Players start with the same number and work down from it, with the objective of reaching zero before their opponents. The goal is crystal clear. There are different ways to reach it, since each turn of three darts produces a different total score via different individual combinations. If there were no number to start from or work toward, each throw would be meaningless. With the goal formulated and defined, however, every single toss of the dart becomes significant, has an effect on the eventual outcome, and influences the strategy of the next moment. As the scores descend, tactics may change multiple times as the players constantly re-evaluate their most efficient path to victory. The end goal, however, stays where it is.

The Four Golden Components of TIME

Goals can be complicated. They should be given the right amount of thought and attention before being committed to. On the other hand, they can also be daunting, tempting us to overthink them and preventing us from working up the nerve to take the plunge. Don't get yourself all twisted wondering if you've defined your goals well and then wasting energy spinning your wheels instead of using it to take action.

Here is a simple acronym – TIME – that serves as an easy checklist to assess whether you've outlined a goal effectively. If you have, it will include:

- ⋏ An explicit **Timeline**. Let's say your goal is to quit smoking – for good this time. There's a big difference between "I will quit smoking" and "I will quit smoking by the end of May." Why is this difference so crucial? Because without a timeline, you can continue not to meet the intended goal, since you always have an out: I can still get it done. If not by the end of May, then by the beginning of fall. If not by then, then by New Year's. If not then, well, maybe it was meant to be the following May all along. There are too many ways to rationalize not meeting a goal, and too many things just waiting to disrupt your progress if you let them. If there's no timeline, there can be no real plan, other than an arbitrary one that can be abandoned anytime, with no true implications. Apply some positive pressure on yourself. Choose a date that's reasonable. Work backward from there. Make a plan. And get going, because no one else is going to do it for you.

- ⋏ A high degree of **Importance**. The goals that feel most intimidating to you are likely the ones you should pursue the hardest, since odds are they're the ones you want the most. It can be difficult to prioritize. You probably have a lot of things you'd like to do and a wide range of goals you imagine achieving. Which are the ones you'd be most disappointed not to meet? Which would count as true missed opportunities, things about which you'd always second-guess yourself, real death-bed regrets? Which represent hobbies or curiosities, and which are deep passions? Which ones do you think about doing just because someone else has done it, as opposed to those which would have an impact on your life, or the lives of your loved ones? Which would be accomplished in isolation, as standalone feats, and which would have a positive domino effect in other parts of your life? It has to matter to you, in a real and substantial way, and it needs to be worthwhile, so that, when you get there, it will truly make a difference in your life.

▲ The ability to be **Measured.** You have to be able to say, I've met this target, or I haven't. There's no gray area. If you can say "I'm kind of meeting this goal," you haven't really defined the goal. Specificity is everything. Lose twenty pounds. Bowl a seventy-five. (I'm not a very good bowler. Hey, it's still a goal.) Complete the treehouse. Visit a city you've never been to. Go hang gliding, skydiving or bungee jumping. Use clear thresholds, concrete numbers, indisputable targets. Without them, you're aiming at nothing.

▲ The requirement of **Effort**. Serious effort. I'm not talking about, for example, buying a pile of lottery tickets as the means to hitting your financial goals. I'm talking about doing something that warrants real exertion, so that, when you succeed, it's matched with an equal level of gratification. Anyone can complete a hundred-meter race. All you need to do is get in the starting blocks. Heck, you can even see the finish line, and the path to get there is already marked. To do it well, though, you need to practice, refine your technique, train your body. You need to build strength and stamina. You need to eat right, rest well, recover properly. To do it better than others, you need to do all those same things to an even greater extent. To be one of the best, you may need to work harder than you've ever worked at anything before. And if the goal is worth it, that's exactly what you'll do.

Defining your goals is the first crucial step to placing them firmly within your conceptual vision and practical grasp. In the next chapter, we'll talk about the plans you need to make in pursuit of that finish line, so you can burst out of the starting blocks and take those first exciting strides.

Nichole's Story

At the age of twenty-one, I was in a serious boating accident. It resulted in the loss of my left leg below the knee, and severe damage to my left hand.

To say it drastically changed my life is an obvious understatement. The biggest impact on me had to do with athletics. I'd always been someone who played sports, excelled at them, and got a rush from the competition, the intensity, and, most of all, the self-challenge.

For a year or so after the accident, I felt like I was in a kind of limbo, or parallel universe. While watching all my friends continue to attend school, play sports, and live normal lives, I was spending my days doing physiotherapy, getting surgeries to repair my hand – seven of them in two years – and traveling far from home to look for a prosthetic that fit. It was as though I'd been pushed to the sidelines of my own life, in which I'd been such a fierce participant before.

That first year was highly draining, deeply frustrating, and extremely challenging, both physically and emotionally. The accident had thrown my life in a new direction. What direction that was, I didn't know, nor how to take the first steps. I didn't know anyone who had experienced something similar, so there was no model to follow, or someone from whom I could seek guidance. And I admit I'm an impatient person at the best of times. This tested my patience, and my perspective, in a way I'd never been tested.

A few things helped me get through. First, my love of sports and my competitive drive helped me focus on getting back onto the field, or diamond, or track. I couldn't wait to return and show everyone what I could accomplish, despite what had happened. Second, there were countless friends and family members who supported me every step of the way. They would take turns joining me for appointments, keeping me focused on the bigger picture, and finding ways to give me a smile or a laugh amid the constant tears. Thanks to them, I was able to avoid slipping into the kind of depression that people often experience after such things happen.

I remember, at a certain point, thinking "I'm not letting this go on much longer." My own internal drive, combined with that amazing support from others rallying around me, had made it possible to persevere, and now I felt ready to take back my life. I finished the rehab on my hand – my middle finger ended up being fused at the knuckle, and I have a big scar all the way down my forearm to the top of my wrist – and I was slowly getting used to the prosthetic. Finally, I felt myself coming out the other side. Most important of all, I could resume playing sports. I remained an athlete to my core, and I was keen to show everyone what I could do. Getting back into that competitive environment allowed me to start reclaiming my sense of self. It gave me new energy, allowed me to find my happiness again.

Coming back into myself also gave me the strength and confidence to pay forward the good deeds others had done to help me through that dark period. I started going to the hospital to visit those who were going through similar situations as I had. Though I didn't lie about how hard it would be or sugar-coat the process, I reassured them there was a light at the end of the tunnel, using myself as an example.

The other way I paid it forward was by chance, and it ended up changing the course of my life. I was playing in a softball tournament and happened to meet a couple whose daughter had lost her leg. They introduced me to her, and through her I discovered a camp for disabled kids that she attended, sponsored by the Amputee Coalition of America. I decided that becoming a chaperone there would be a great way for me to give back. I introduced the campers to different adaptive sports and at the same time discovered those sports myself, including wheelchair basketball, sled hockey, and sitting volleyball. That one intrigued me the most. I'd loved volleyball before the accident, but conventional ("standing") volleyball was now a lot more challenging for me. Sitting volleyball was a whole new, and exciting, way for me to play the sport.

Less than a year later, I found myself trying out for the U.S. Women's Sitting Volleyball Team, and earning a spot. It opened a whole new world for me, allowing me to travel the globe, meet other like-minded athletes, and immerse myself in sports again, on a bigger stage than I would ever have dreamed.

During my first couple of years on the team, I continued living in my hometown of Champaign, Illinois, working as a legal secretary. In 2007, a year ahead of the Beijing Paralympics, I decided to move to Edmond, Oklahoma, where the team's main training facility is located. I quit my job, sold my house, found an apartment, and began training more seriously. I also enrolled at the University of Central Oklahoma, where I would finish my Bachelor's degree, then an MBA as well.

Training full-time helped me excel at the sport and reach my peak. I'd started it older than most do – just before my twenty-eighth birthday – so I was determined to be the best I could and contribute to the team as much as possible. In 2008, we reached the final, losing to China and earning silver. Four years later, at the London Olympics, China defeated us for gold again. I moved back home to Champaign and found a job in the environmental field, a passion of mine. Though I remained a part of the team, I was no longer training at the same level as before, so it became more difficult to keep my edge. Now I had an even more enriching role: that of veteran and mentor to the other players. While my own competitive spirit continued to burn, being able to give advice and encouragement to others was even more gratifying. In 2016, at the Rio de Janeiro Games, we faced China in the finals for a third consecutive time – and this time broke through, taking gold. It was an unforgettable moment, one that gave me the dual joy of being both a player and a leader.

When the Tokyo Games approached in 2020, I looked forward to defending the gold we'd finally won. Then Covid hit, and there was a year-long delay. During that period, most of my teammates continued to train full-time at the facility in Oklahoma, and continued to improve. Fast-forward to July 2021 – I was told I didn't make the Paralympic roster. It was a blow. I felt I could still contribute, especially in my role as veteran, leader and mentor. Managing my disappointment was extremely difficult. This had been the most important thing in my life for the past sixteen and a half years, and now it had come to an abrupt end.

Then a month later, just before the team was preparing to leave, one of the girls on the team unfortunately tested positive for Covid. I was asked to step in for her. Of course I agreed. This sport, and this team, had given me so much, and I wasn't about to let them down. I was forty-four, and I knew it would be my last go-round. I would give it everything I had.

When we finally reached Tokyo in August 2021 after the long Covid delay, we started slowly, losing to China in the round robin. Pulling together, we beat Brazil in the semis to reach the finals and meet our old foes yet again. That day, we played the best match of our lives, defending the gold. What a way to go out.

Chapter 4: Chart the Course

Have you ever played with LEGO? Using those little interlocking plastic blocks of different shapes, sizes and colors, one can create a seemingly infinite variety of things, limited only by imagination. (This is virtually true; six 2 x 4 bricks can be combined in 915,103,765 ways.)

What I've always found most interesting about LEGO, though, is the popularity of the pre-designed sets. From princess castles to space robots, from the Millennium Falcon to the Taj Mahal, people love building the sets even if they already know how they're going to look when finished – actually, *especially* when they already know.

Jigsaw puzzles represent the same phenomenon. Watch someone spending hours putting together a LEGO set or poring over a thousand-piece jigsaw puzzle for multiple nights and you're watching the same instinct in action. If you give children a bunch of LEGO pieces and just watch them create, it's wonderful. Notice the difference in focus and energy, however, when it's a pre-fab set and they know what it's going to be when they're done. Watch the growing anticipation (interspersed with moments of frustration, and probably a decent number of expletives) in someone getting closer to solidifying a jigsaw puzzle. The thrill of getting to the finish line is enough to make them spend all that back-stiffening time at the dining room table, skipping meals and ignoring the family – even though they already know what it's going to look like.

Yes, the most enjoyable way for us to reach an end point is via a predetermined path. Our great satisfaction comes not from arriving at the end to find a surprise; it comes from completing the set, or picture, that we had in mind all along.

In the previous chapter, we covered defining your goals clearly in order to pursue them effectively. Now let's talk about making plans to achieve those goals – LEGO-like plans, jigsaw puzzle-type plans, where the endpoint is known, the steps are clear, and every step moves you forward.

The Practical

When you make plans to reach your goals, you enable your own abilities. You facilitate your own talents. You empower yourself to achieve while, to the extent possible, removing the impact of unknowns. Making a plan to reach a goal doesn't make that goal any less special; it simply places it in operable terms. As an important mentor in my life, Ben Kinney, once said, "Dream long-term. Set goals for the short term. Take action now."

Planning has a profound effect on both the effectiveness with which you pursue a goal and the comfort level you have while doing so. The difference between following a plan and flying by the seat of your pants is the difference between getting on a plane knowing your destination and strapping in having no idea where you might end up. Once you've defined your goal, the next step is obvious: designing the plan to meet it. While doing so, keep these three principles in mind:

▲ **Keep it simple.** People love doing elaborate presentations, showing off complicated schematics, and sharing pages of heavily detailed strategic documents packed with sections, sub-sections and sub-sub-sections. They adore their pivot tables and decision trees. They're into critical paths, pie charts, project planners, frameworks and paradigms. I get it – these things look fancy, seem impressive and imply a high volume of effort in the high degree of complexity.

They are also usually padded with a lot of superfluous and unnecessary stuff. When creating plans to meet your goals, focus on what really matters, and don't distract yourself with extraneous stuff – quality over quantity should be your guiding mantra. Overly complicated plans cause fatigue at best, confusion at worst. Strip it to the essentials and make the steps clear. It's common that plans are created yet nothing is done, because the plan itself is so convoluted that it feels more like a maze. Simple is powerful.

Here's what you don't need: lots of colors, different shapes, tons of arrows, bulleted lists of dependencies, SWOT analyses (strengths, weaknesses, opportunities, threats), tiny unreadable fonts in the attempt to jam pages full of information. Here's what you do need: at the top, your ultimate goal; below it, the steps required to reach that goal, a deadline for each step, a bit of detail for each one if necessary, and a space where you check off the steps as you complete them. Those are the elements of a good plan. Don't crowd the path with unwanted sticks and pebbles that impede your way and block your view of the finish line. Keep it as clear as possible.

Think about a game of checkers versus chess. In both, you know the objective. However, in checkers, the way to achieve it is far simpler, whereas chess involves nearly infinite scenarios. Most people would probably say that the intricacy of chess is what makes it so fascinating and compelling. However, it's also why so many games end in stalemates. In checkers, the range of movement is highly limited. In chess, even individual pieces can go in different directions. Stick with the checkers mentality.

▲ **Make it actionable.** Plans are not a collection of ideas and thoughts; they are a list of things to *do*. They are practicable, implementable, easy to dive into, ready to be executed. Plans of *action*, not of description.

Let's say the goal is to conquer your fear of spiders. The steps might include talking to friends who have overcome similar fears, reading about the phobia to understand how you might have acquired it in the first place (though I'm pretty sure I got it sitting in the second row while watching the movie *Arachnophobia*), and undergoing Cognitive Behavioral Therapy. There you go – schedule those steps. Know who you're going to call and what you're going to read. Understand how long that type of therapy usually takes and research those who provide it. Bake the steps into the plan, then get going on it. Say your goal is to lose fifteen pounds in the next three months. That might entail eliminating red meat, limiting French fries to the first Tuesday of each month, and drinking half your body weight in ounces of water every day. List the components, then bear down. Want to finish the first draft of your screenplay? Estimate how many pages it will be in total. Decide how many of those you're going to write each day, for how many days, starting tomorrow, with no revising allowed. Then do it.

▲ **Break it down.** The distance between the start and the end can seem long, and, sometimes, demoralizing without the feeling of progress and momentum along the way. Apply to your own plan the same advice you give your child regarding a big school project: break it down into manageable chunks. Don't worry about the finish line. It's there. No need to look too far ahead when you begin. Create goals that build upon each other. Identify reasonable thresholds to pass and milestones to hit as you go, so that you aren't focused only on the big goal, which can feel nebulous and ungraspable until you get close to it. In the previous chapter, we discussed, as one example of a clearly defined goal, someone aiming to become anchor of their top regional news station within a decade. That's a terrific long-term aim – which will require a number of short-term steps along the way.

Including these stepwise, incremental goals works no matter how big or small the ultimate objective. Terry Fox, in his quest to help raise funds for cancer research, aimed to run from one coast of Canada to the other by completing the equivalent of a marathon per day on his one good leg and one prosthetic leg – and had somehow been achieving this feat for a mind-boggling one hundred and forty-three days before his cancer tragically returned, interrupting the run forever. Roger Bannister (yes, another runner; forgive me, I really love running) didn't just step on the track one day and attempt to run the first sub-four-minute mile. He constructed a specific plan breaking down the race into sections, knowing that if he knocked off each one in order, success would be the outcome. Even hundred-meter sprinters divide their race into four distinct phases – start, acceleration, transition, and maximum velocity – training for each one in highly customized ways before knitting the run together.

By assigning periodic goals, you create periodic wins, reinforcing your confidence and assurance to continue. This is important because different objectives will involve different rates of change, some quicker and more frequent, some slower and more spread out. If you have a significant amount of weight to lose, you'll likely start seeing changes soon after making even small adjustments to your diet and exercise. If you're wanting to get rid of those last ten pounds, progress will probably be more the slow-and-steady kind. Building in milestones helps you not get too high during periods of noticeable change or rapid progress and not get too low doing those times when you're laying the foundation for change and doing the work nobody else sees. Every part of the plan matters and none of it is to be ignored. Build it well. Follow it diligently. Watch the results happen.

The Mental

Defining a goal takes thinking; executing the plan to meet that goal takes effort. If you've created the plan properly, implementing it will tax you, because it will require ongoing energy, sustained focus, and continuous determination. When goals are abandoned rather than met, it isn't usually a matter of plans being poor, resources insufficient, or steps unclear. It's more often because someone simply lost the heart for it or ran out of gas. The ultimate prize felt too far away, too impossible to reach, or the obstacles too big to surmount.

The stick-to-it-iveness needed to reach your big goals is as much about the mental task as it is the practical one. Here are three principles for getting in the right frame of mind at the start, and keeping it going till the finish.

- ▲ **Go hard.** It doesn't make sense to go after anything half-heartedly. Do it all the way or don't do it at all. If you want to reach the top of a mountain, you don't put on a pair of sneakers and casually hike up a random trail. You choose a specific route, assemble the proper gear, steel yourself for the exertion, and get after it. When it gets hard, you keep going.

    In sports like tennis or golf, where the top hundred players are extremely similar in skill, how many times have you heard commentators say that those who win consistently do so because of their mental makeup or ability to master the emotional game? Everyone has a game plan going in; those whose mental will matches it tend to emerge from the pack. Heed the words of Les Brown: "If you set goals and go after them with all the determination you can muster, your gifts will take you places that will amaze you." Or the slightly less elegant yet no less accurate words of Mike Tyson: "Everybody has a plan until they get punched in the mouth." Though the delivery of these two is a bit different, both are giving us the same advice. Set your goals, make your plans, and stick with them (even if you get punched in the mouth – figuratively, I would hope). Put your head down, take a deep breath, and pursue it with all the gusto you possess.

▲ **Take breaks.** No one can go full-tilt all the time. Even the most hardcore exercise regimens include rest days. Twenty-minute power naps do wonders for energy and focus. The Beatles paused their breakneck recording pace to chill out in India.

You likewise need to build in time to restore and recharge. A brief meditation session every day, in the same spot, no exceptions. A walk on the trail near your home or a stroll to buy something from one of the local retailers. A game of tennis with a friend. Watching a movie. Reading. Whatever suits you best. Make it (a) regular, (b) consistent and (c) timed. That third part is the most important. Watching two episodes of a show you like is a good break. Reaching the end of the week and realizing you're behind on your plan because you binged the entirety of Game of Thrones is not (although it sure was great, at least until that last season).

▲ **Visualize the finish.** As you go, keep reminding yourself that the end result will be a culmination of all the effort you've put in leading to that point. Success seldom happens overnight. The star athlete who "came out of nowhere" probably put in thousands of hours of pre-dawn training before you ever heard their name. The movie star that "had a mercurial rise to fame" likely did more auditions than you can count and endured more failed pilots than you can name before landing the gig that put them on the map. Odds are the inventor who "struck it rich" with the brilliant new innovation that everyone is buying persevered through innumerable disasters and dead ends before landing on that magazine cover.

In the end, you're the only person who can do this, so you need to imagine how it's going to feel when you cross the tape. What is it going to mean when you get there? I don't mean what it's going to do for you practically; I mean think about how it's going to feel. Close your eyes and picture it. Capture in your mind, your heart, your body, what that feeling will be. Anticipate it in the most tangible way you can, even though you aren't there yet. You know you're going to do it. You're going to get there. It's going to be amazing. And, yes, it will sure feel great to let others know you've accomplished that goal. You know what's going to be an even better moment? Looking in the mirror and saying, *You did it.*

Jason's Story

Growing up, I was always given choices. My dad expected me to keep up in school, and at the same time he encouraged me to explore interests in music, art, sports – whatever might strike my fancy. As a professional drummer, he appreciated the idea of finding one's own path, whether or not it was the conventional one. The only thing he did want me to think about was goal-setting. Whatever it was I might decide to pursue, he urged me to define a series of small goals as stepping stones to achieving larger ones. Regardless of the context, he would ask me questions like, *What do you want to accomplish? And what are the steps that will get you there?* Learning to lay out interim and end goals in that way helped me build confidence, and gave me the belief that I could aim high, and be smart and strategic in meeting those aims.

Toward the end of high school, I still didn't have a clear passion, or a specific idea of what I wanted to do, or be. College wasn't particularly calling to me, and no brilliant entrepreneurial bulbs were going off in my mind. My best friend told me his dad needed someone to help in the kitchen at his restaurant in Long Island. That seemed as good an option as anything else I could think of at the time. It was an eye-opening experience, and very hard work, requiring twelve-to-sixteen-hour days. I was up for it, since I'd always been active and was pretty fit as a result, so energy and stamina weren't a problem.

What did become a problem was being around all that food – and drink. When I started the job, I weighed about 195 pounds. After a year, I'd somehow ballooned to over 300. It happened almost without my realizing it, a bit at a time, a few pounds here and there. I was working those long hours and then always eating at the end of my shifts – far too late, and far too much. The drinking was worse than the eating. Food puts on the pounds in an obvious way; alcohol is sneakier.

When I discovered how heavy I'd become, I was shocked, even though the evidence was right there in the mirror day after day. It's remarkable what we can ignore, or at least choose not to deal with. I didn't know how I'd reached this point. I could barely make it up the stairs without losing my breath. I decided it was time to do something about it.

One day, I was on the phone with a close friend who lived in Colorado. I confided to him about how big I'd gotten and the dangerous spot I'd put myself in. He was cool about it – supportive without being judgmental. Out of the blue, he suggested I come to Vail. Not visit Vail; move there. I told him I didn't know anything about Vail. "What do you need to know?" he said. "One, you love snowboarding. Two, you need a change." It was actually a pretty good argument. Without thinking twice, I decided to move across the country.

Despite my terrible physical state, when I arrived in Colorado, I felt exhilarated at the prospect of a fresh start and unknown possibilities. Breathing that clean mountain air, waking up to those stunning views – all of it inspired me to get off on the right foot. The true motivating moment involved a foot indeed – my friend's. I was hiking with him one afternoon when, coming down a hill, I stumbled forward because of the size of my stomach, and stepped on his foot, fracturing one of the bones. It would have been embarrassing enough on its own; worse, my friend was a tennis instructor. I felt terrible. As I said, he'd been cool about my negative spiral, expressing no judgment. Now he got a little more direct. "Jay," he said, "I love you like a brother, but you're fat. Whatever's going on with you, you need to figure it out." That tough love was exactly what I needed. All I said back was "Thank you."

That evening, I thought back to the conversations with my dad about setting goals and making plans for reaching them. I wanted to do him proud, and to reclaim my former self. I looked at the calendar on the wall. Today was April 20. My eye went three months forward to the last day of spring, June 20, and without thinking, on that date I wrote the number 195 – my previous weight. Then I did the calculation: three months to lose a little over a hundred pounds. I had no idea whether it was possible. I was going to give it my best shot regardless.

The next morning, I put my car in storage and bought a mountain bike. From that moment on, I vowed to walk, run or bike everywhere I needed to go, rain or shine. That was the first promise I made to myself in pursuit of the larger goal of getting back to my old weight. I'd learned, from succeeding at other things, and from my dad's guidance, that setting those smaller, reachable objectives can help position you to achieve big things, and can also allow you to pivot, adapt and stay resilient when things change, as they inevitably do.

Every other decision I made, I made with a view toward that larger goal. I enrolled online to become certified as a fitness trainer. I got a job as a personal trainer in a nearby country club, which kept me on my feet and moving around throughout the day. I told my best friend, and the other new friends I'd made, about my goal, so that they could support and challenge me, especially when we went out. I started doing daily bike rides along the many trails in the town where the club was located, a village called Beaver Creek and one of the most beautiful places I'd ever been in. The charming alpine setting, the active outdoor culture, and the friendly, laid-back environment all spoke to me. In this place, I felt like I could get back to the person I was, or at least had been.

In those 91 days, I kept to my smaller goals – took the bike everywhere, started eating well, got certified as a fitness instructor, spent lots of time in the pure mountain air of Beaver Creek. Doing those positive, productive acts day after day helped them become regular habits, and then something like muscle memory. On June 19, the second-last day of spring, the day before the day I'd circled on my calendar, I worked my shift at the country club, played some pickup basketball, and took a nice evening ride around town on my bike. The next morning, I got on the scale, and saw the number flicker for a moment, then settle at 195.

Since hitting that goal, I haven't let myself go back to the insidious habits that at one time led to such a bad place. My incentive has changed over time. In that first period, it was to rediscover the person I'd been and turn my life around. Later, when I got married and had kids, it was to make sure I'd be around for my family for a long time, be able to take care of them mentally, physically and financially, and always be an active, involved father.

Today, at forty-seven and a dad of three, I continue to set goals, typically using a 3-6-9 structure whereby I set milestones for three, six and nine months out. Having kids creates a whole new set of demands and responsibilities, and, just like when I worked in my friend's restaurant as a teen, it could be easy for me to let myself slip, since a lot of my time is now occupied by things like cooking dinner, doing laundry, washing dishes, and watching TV or movies together. I record my big goals as well as my smaller ones, and then I put them on sticky notes, on the mirror, on the fridge, to remind myself of them every day and put in the work. When I hit those goals, I set new ones, to make sure I'm constantly forcing myself out of whatever new comfort zone I've reached. I make the goals reasonable yet also tough, so that it feels worthwhile when I attain them.

We only get one shot at life. When things get hard, or complicated, or daunting, I take a moment to remember what my dad taught me, and those questions he'd ask. *What do you want to accomplish? And what are the steps that will get you there?*

Chapter 5: Think, Then Act

We've talked about optimizing your environment and creating the conditions for success; maximizing your strengths while managing your weaknesses; defining your goals; and laying effective paths to reach them. The pursuit of these goals requires you to weigh options and make decisions – lots of them, at every stage. For some of those decisions, you might evaluate different possibilities for weeks. Others may take virtually no time at all. Achieving your apex means, among other things, being efficient about the information you gather and decisive about the actions you take.

Patience and Purpose

Think about the amount of information you take in and the number of decisions you make while driving. Every moment you're behind that wheel, you're calculating speed and direction (at least I hope you are), measuring your position relative to other cars, checking mirrors, scanning for cyclists or pedestrians, anticipating the pattern of stoplights, and so much more.

Apex animals are the same, processing large amounts of information constantly. However, instead of doing so for the purpose of grocery shopping, going to the movies or meeting a friend for dinner, they do so to ensure safety and find sustenance.

These exceptional animals tend to have two things in common. The first is patience: they wait, lurk and observe, silently collecting information to maximize their likelihood of success. The second is purpose: when they act, they do so efficiently and decisively, wasting neither time nor movement.

We can see these twin attributes at work in various apex predators. Eagles sit on their perches waiting, watching, until the time is right to swoop and strike. Saltwater crocodiles bide their time underwater, using special nerve endings on their jaws and the undersides of their bodies to detect a potential meal approaching the water's edge. Tigers stalk their prey slowly and carefully, often waiting from the rear before making their lethal move. Polar bears, their fur acting as camouflage against the ice and snow, creep up on sunbathing seals, finding just the right position from

49

which to pounce. Lions will sometimes stalk their prey for hours before deciding to pounce. (I've spent considerable time at the sandwich counter before making a decision – though I'd agree that lions' stakes are a bit higher.)

Part of the reason apex animals display such an impressive combination of patience and purpose is that they have little choice. Their biological instincts remind them every moment how crucial both traits are, and that a slight tactical miscalculation can mean the difference between catching a meal and having it escape. When planning our next meal, we look in the fridge, go to the grocery store, or order take-out. These creatures, though they sit at the top of the food chain, face, in nature itself, a daily obstacle greater than any other predator, and because of it, must employ extreme focus and strategy in the pursuit of every meal, one involving a subtle balance of waiting, then acting.

In a sense, it's easier to base every decision on biological instinct. We, by contrast, are often subject to pesky nuisances like feelings, biases, memories and reflection. While the ability to pause, consider and analyze can be an advantage, it can also be a serious obstacle. As humans, we're susceptible to two types of errors: acting on too much information, or too little. Excitement, compulsion or temptation can make us jump the gun. Anxiety, uncertainty or confusion can freeze us in place. Those who perform at an apex level rarely take premature action, yet they also seldom get caught spinning their wheels. How do you attain that level, and stay there consistently?

The Case of the Dad Who Lost It

Leading up to my daughter Simone's birth, I, like most parents, was eager to sponge as much information as I could in order to become an amazing father, or at least avoid being responsible for the death of my daughter. At a friend's suggestion, I read *What To Expect When You're Expecting*…which made *The Shining* look like a nursery rhyme. I came away from it not exactly assured of my parenting ability. It would be more accurate to say I was confident my child was certain to die within hours of our bringing her home, if she was lucky enough to even make it out of the hospital.

Despite the book's ominous (and countless) warnings about what could go wrong, we managed to keep our daughter in one piece for her first six weeks. We lived in Las Vegas, and I had a job in one of the stage shows which didn't get me home until about midnight, when I would give Simone her midnight bottle, then put her in her crib to sleep. Still wired, I'd typically watch a movie or a baseball rebroadcast, then give Simone her 3:00 a.m. bottle. Her mom would then wake up to feed her at 6:00 a.m., and so on, both of us getting whatever snatches of sleep we could. We'd settled into as much of a routine as new parents can.

On one of these nights, I'd given Simone her midnight feeding and was watching a baseball game while checking on her constantly. (All parents will be familiar with this.) As 3:00 a.m. neared, I didn't hear anything from her crib. (All parents of newborns will also understand that there are two things equally distressing from one's baby. One is noise. The other is no noise.)

I put my ear to the baby monitor – nothing. I waited three minutes. Still nothing. Quickly entering panic mode, I went to her and did the test the book had taught me: lift a foot and gently let it go to see if the child responds. I did; she didn't. The book advised me to do the same with the baby's arm, which I did three times, imagining that on the third I would see her arm remain suspended and she would wag her finger Hulk Hogan-style. Instead, her arm fell three times. Gear-shifting into abject terror, I snatched her, raced downstairs, secured her in her car seat, and broke a variety of laws on the way to the hospital.

I can't remember if I turned the car off as I screeched into the Emergency entrance, yanked out the baby seat with Simone still in it, and ran inside screaming for someone to help. One nurse grabbed the car seat from me while another asked me questions and handed me forms.

After what felt like an eternity during which my mind went to the darkest places, finally a doctor came out holding Simone, who was awake and seemed her normal self.

"Is this your daughter?" the doctor said.

"Yes," I replied.

"Congratulations on waking her up," he said. "And good luck getting her back to sleep."

What I'd discovered was that, at six weeks, my daughter was ready to sleep through the night.

51

For new parents, emotions and exhaustion rule while intellect and rationality take a back seat. It is darn near impossible for a new parent to consider information intelligently and dispassionately. Freaking out about everything is practically a hallmark of first-time parenting. (So in that way, I was a model dad!) I'd amassed so much information that, in the process, I'd lost all reason. I hadn't merely absorbed the book's information; I'd absorbed it, intensified it, and inflated it so much that information had become fear.

I did one thing right in that situation: I acted. What I did wrong was basing that action on just one source of information and allowing my decisions to be fueled only by emotions. When learning within a new context, one ought to seek information in various places. I was in unfamiliar mental and emotional territory, looking up from the bottom of a large learning curve. I was impressionable to any advice from anyone.

What should I have done? Collected more information, from a wider range of sources, so that, once in that sleep-deprived and anxious state, I could have had a better chance of thinking about which of them to act on when stressful moments like this did arise. I could have at least read *two* books.

A Shark's Focus

In the example above, I got my information from only one source, became overwhelmed by possible negative scenarios as a result, and freaked out accordingly. I was a great example of acting narrowly.

On the other hand, is there such a thing as collecting too much data to help inform decisions? Perhaps you've heard the expression "analysis paralysis," which describes a phenomenon in which too much thinking results in no action. This syndrome is illustrated by the famous fable "The Fox and the Cat," in which a fox boasts to a cat about the many ways it can escape trouble, while the cat replies that it has just one. When hunters soon arrive with their hounds, the cat quickly dashes up a tree, while the fox, considering its numerous options, gets caught. The fable concludes with the moral, "Better one safe way than a hundred on which you cannot reckon." In other words, sometimes we need to spend less time thinking and more time acting.

Of course, it can be risky to jump at the first piece of information we find, since it doesn't usually provide the full picture. Did you know that polar bears are not, in fact, white? We see them that way due to a trick of the light. A polar bear's individual hairs are actually free of pigment – and because of this transparency, they scatter and reflect visible light the same way ice and snow do, making them look white to us.

In a similar way, we can get distracted by misleading perspectives, preventing us from seeing in a focused way and assimilating information effectively. In the course of gathering information and considering it from different angles, we can again take lessons from apex animals, who are experts at cutting through the irrelevant and taking focused action. Great white sharks, for example, can detect one drop of blood in about twenty-six gallons of water. No wonder they're such fearsome hunters. Sometimes it's hard to cut through the noise of all the information we're bombarded with on a daily basis today to focus on what matters. Those able to do so consistently are those who realize greater success.

The Action Sweet Spot

So on one hand, we often do things like clicking "Buy now" on Amazon out of pure impulse, for items we hardly need. (Nita and I use a system she brilliantly suggested whereby we agree to wait forty-eight hours after adding any item to our Amazon cart before confirming the purchase. Thanks to her, many unnecessary or impulse items end up being discarded.) On the other hand, we just as often spend so much time thinking about decisions that we never get around to making them. In this way, it certainly does seem easier to be a lion or crocodile and not have the chance (or the time) to create pro-con lists or perform a risk-reward analysis. Everything is instinct and action. Apex animals prepare and then pounce; they learn, then they leap.

So how do you achieve the controlled spontaneity and informed decisiveness of apex performers? What's the right formula?

It depends – on your objectives, your situation, your circumstances, and, most important, your individual makeup. Some people benefit from extra time to think and reflect; some get easily stuck. I might be the type of person who likes to bounce things off others; you might be more of a lone wolf. One person may be confident in their intuition and comfortable following their gut; a different person may prefer to ignore hunches and trust the facts.

Just as we discussed in the chapter about finding your unique mix of strengths, there is no standard equation for how much information you should assemble before making a decision, or how long you should digest it before taking action. The balance is specific to you. We all learn at different speeds; we absorb information in different ways, at different rates; we experience different emotions that affect our decision-making.

What's critical is to be aware of the need for both patience and purpose. The more you practice both these sides of the coin when facing decisions, the more natural the process will become, and the more easily you'll discover the approach that leads to your apex level. Will you always act at exactly the right time, in precisely the right way? Of course not. Your goal should not be a perfect track record – that's impossible. Lions and crocs don't always succeed, either. Your goal should be to improve over time, zeroing in more and more on the balance that works best for you. Gather information thoroughly. Consider it properly. Act decisively. And enjoy the results.

Chelsea's Story

My story started in Portland in my early twenties. I had a healthy wanderlust and wanted to explore somewhere new – somewhere away from home, though not too far away. My first job there was in a gorgeous tequila bar. I embraced the service industry culture with open arms. While the long shifts could be brutal, the weekends always brought a party or opportunity to travel. Free tequila tastings to become "experts" in our industry didn't hurt, either. It was here that drinking and working started to become intermingled for me. Friends and patrons in the environment were working hard and partying harder, a sentiment I got behind easily – too easily.

After a few years of working and playing, I decided to seek a career in real estate. In an eye-blink, I'd been thrust into a world where the norm was working sixty hours a week – some weeks, closer to eighty. It got to the point where I would be at my desk before the sun rose and then leave around ten p.m., thinking nothing of it.

This extreme environment allowed me to grow and change at a record-breaking pace, both positively and negatively. Because I was glued to my work, I hardly went outside. When I did, it was to smoke. I ate a lot of fast food and take-out. The work-hard, play-hard lifestyle hadn't gone away, though. My closest colleague and I would go to her house after work and drink vodka cranberries, continuing to work late into the night. We had big visions to execute, and had to find ways to make the insurmountable tasks we'd been assigned "fun."

The progression was subtle – to me, at least. It's easy to fall victim to it, especially at that age, when you're more vulnerable to that kind of pressure and more likely to act in a conforming way. It was always work, socialize, drink, repeat.

One fateful day, I finally decided to leave the job and escape that environment. Unfortunately, by that point, drinking had become so rooted in my day that it didn't slow down. Even though I was aware how bad it had become, I was unable to stop. I have four years' worth of journal entries that contain variations of the phrases, *I will be sober*, *I can do it* and *I can quit*. Yet I couldn't.

The issue was that, even though I'd had this revelation that I truly wanted to quit, I didn't have any evidence that I could. So instead of jumping right into a program that I was, in my experience, destined to fail, I decided to do some evidence-gathering first, hoping it would help me make a plan and put me in a better position to succeed.

I remembered a story I'd heard, a fable, about an old man who goes to his backyard every morning and rolls a big boulder across it, to the opposite, farthest corner of the yard. After many days of this, his family asks him, "Why are you doing this every morning? Have you lost your mind?"

"I roll this boulder every day," he tells them, "to prove to myself that I can overcome a challenge every day."

I said to myself, I have to find my boulder, some small act or behavior that can show me I'm capable of making a conscious change. I'd plunged into huge pursuits before and failed, which had only made me feel worse about myself. At one point, for example, I'd attempted a specific program in which one must satisfy five components every day – drink a gallon of water, stick to a specific diet (with no alcohol or cheat meals), work out twice a day for forty-five minutes each (one of which must be outdoors), read ten pages of a self-help or entrepreneurial book, and take a progress photo. My taking that on was like going from couch potato to marathon runner overnight. The funny thing is I actually achieved the alcohol part of it, not taking a drink for seventy-five days. Then I celebrated by getting drunk on champagne. I questioned myself yet again. *Why are you doing all this work and modeling self-discipline just to then go back to what is essentially the starting point?*

Finally, I hit bottom one day. Or rather, one night – New Year's Eve. I got extremely drunk and ended up vomiting in my friend's driveway to ring in the new year. I was so embarrassed. I remember thinking, I'm thirty, I'm this awful mess doing this in a driveway in a nice neighborhood on a night that's supposed to mean change and hope for what's to come. I asked myself, *Is this how you want people to see you? To remember you? Is this the picture you want them to have?*

I was fed up with myself, and my own excuses. I decided to quit drinking.

This time I knew I would succeed. What made my decision different from the years prior was that I finally had the evidence I needed. In the months before, I had started building evidence by focusing on a small challenge to do every day. I carefully chose something I could do for myself that I could point to whenever I started to doubt my own ability to create change. I had my very own boulder. The simplest challenge I could think of: walking.

I got super specific with it. I decided I would walk every day, come rain, sun or snow. It didn't matter how long I walked; it only mattered that I did. The day I made that decision, I went for a walk. Then the day after, too. And the day after that. Every day, it got a bit easier, and every day, my confidence in myself grew because I had honored my own promise.

I kept it up for just over a month. That was my evidence. I now knew I had the ability to choose to do something and show up. If I could walk every day, I could start not drinking every day, too.

At the same time, I started doing research and reading books on the subject of quitting. Books by experts, testimonials by those who'd succeeded, anything I could get my hands on to feel informed and prepared. Taking on a habit like walking, I knew, was a lot easier than breaking a habit like drinking. I was scared. At the same time, I believed I could do it.

I did something else that proved crucial, something suggested in one of the books I read: creating a plan around what failing would mean. It helped me understand the reasons behind my wanting to achieve this goal, and also change the self-loathing dialogue that had been the main reason for my vicious cycle. For so long, I hadn't quit because failing meant that I saw myself yet again as a bad person with no self-control. I'd bludgeon myself with those kinds of messages, and when I kept failing, it just reinforced this view. I'd created the narrative that this is just who I am, someone who inherently can't change. Obviously we can all change. I'd come to dislike myself so much that I wasn't able to see it.

So this time I committed to creating a plan about what I'd do if I faltered, such as giving myself a day and then starting again, or writing about why it happened, or calling a friend. These are all simple alternatives to the terrible ongoing self-flagellation I'd engaged in. Creating the plan in this more positive and self-loving way gave me a new kind of mental strength and internal belief. Instead of my usual self-punishment spiral, I focused on the positives. I thought about that month during which I'd walked every day and reminded myself that I can change.

After hitting rock bottom on that New Year's night, I decided I was going to stop drinking for a year. To increase the accountability, I shared my intention on social media. Unfortunately, along with a lot of messages of support, the trolls immediately came out, too, including a girl who took me to task for having used the word "sober" in my video. She said I should learn the difference between being sober and just being dry, the difference being, she said, that people who are dry are choosing recreationally not to imbibe. People who are sober have overcome addiction and understand the trauma of alcohol abuse. They don't have a choice. This is the only way they can truly live.

Listening to her rant, something interesting happened to me. At first, I was hurt. I'm attempting to do this life-changing challenge, and some random person attacks me for it. I found myself arguing with her in my mind. *I'm insensitive to sober people, really? You don't know what I've been through. You don't know my trauma. How dare you?* Then I paused and thought about it. I am overcoming addiction. I do have trauma. I can't commit to being dry for a year. I need to commit to a life of sobriety.

I found myself feeling grateful toward her, because she'd made me realize that I was in fact on a path toward being not just dry, but indeed sober. I could now feel that I wasn't resisting the act of picking up a drink; I was avoiding it for the purpose of no longer poisoning my body and my soul. I had chosen to leave my demons behind. She was right – doing one is a lot harder than doing the other. She'd helped me realize that I'd come to a place where I could close that door for good. I've now closed it, and it remains locked behind me, forever.

Chapter 6: Distinguish Competition from Cooperation

We're made to compete. For food, for resources, for space, for status, for survival. In our ancestors' earliest days, competition ruled virtually every moment, and the consequences were almost always life-or-death. Steadily, although our fundamental instincts to compete remained intact, it was when we figured out how to start working together that major leaps began to occur – making fire, hunting in groups, taming the land, planting and harvesting crops, crossing oceans, starting new societies.

Today, the primitive urge to compete still drives us, combined with the more sophisticated awareness of cooperation. When we're behaving at our most evolved, we're combining the two, each person using their instinctive competitive drive to make individual gains while at the same time contributing to the accomplishments of the greater whole.

In our modern world, both competition and cooperation are critical, at levels very small, very large, and everything in between. Over millennia, we've continued to compete and cooperate in ever-expanding ways. The two are connected more often than they aren't, and understanding which is important at what times plays a significant role in performing your best, achieving your most, and pursuing individual goals while serving the collective good.

Competition

In the next chapter, we'll discuss circumstances in which it makes sense to look out for your own interests and act in a way that might be termed "selfish." Are you competing in a small field directly against others hoping to accomplish similar goals, with a small pool of supply – customers, readers, viewers, buyers, partners – to go around? In such situations, it's appropriate to act with self-interest, since you're truly competing for yourself. If competition is on one side of the spectrum and cooperation is on the other, this type of scenario sits at the far end of the competition side. In such a case, the thing to do is put your head down and outwork your competition (while playing fair, or at least within the law – even if you sometimes break unwritten rules). Be better, smarter, more creative, more resilient. Do what it takes to get a foothold. Leverage every possibility at your disposal to build your network, broaden your contacts, market your offerings. Those who reach the top levels of their chosen endeavors in individual pursuits don't shy away from competition; they welcome it.

Don't think of this type of competition as the need to defeat others. Think of it as a challenge to do your own personal best. And remember that, when one person competes hard, others are challenged to do the same, and often end up grateful for being motivated to do so. When one person wins the sales competition for a given quarter, the others on the team likely outperform their previous numbers, too, by virtue of the competition, even if they didn't "win." In truth, everyone won, despite one individual selling the most on the team. Competition raises the collective bar, whether or not we recognize an individual victor.

In fact, whenever you think you're technically competing against others, you're almost always competing against yourself. Why? Because you may think your goal is beating someone else's time, or numbers, or sales, however to do that, you're striving to improve your own results – which is, after all, the only aspect of competition you can control. The presence of others may provide motivation. The competition is with yourself.

Here's an example of what I mean. Gaetan Boucher is a now-famous Canadian speed skater. He competed in his first Olympics in 1976 at Innsbruck at the age of eighteen, finishing in sixth place in the thousand-meter race. In 1980, at the Olympics in Lake Placid, now twenty-two years old, he placed second in the same event.

Over the next four years, Gaetan continued to train hard, working with his coach to refine his technique, skate as efficiently and aerodynamically as possible, maintain form throughout the race, and conserve optimal energy for the punishing kick. When the 1984 Olympics in Sarajevo arrived, he knew he was skating his best, though he didn't know how his best measured up to the elite skaters from other nations. (You need to cast your mind back to a time before social media, YouTube and the instant and continuous news cycle, when things about others weren't as readily known.)

As the competition began and Boucher sat in the training room, awaiting his turn as the others skated two at a time, his coach said something to him – once, twice, then repeatedly: *None of their times are as fast as yours.* As one skater after another finished and the times flashed,

Boucher realized that the competition he had waged with himself over those four years had brought him to a point where his times were superior to all others in the world. All he needed to do was skate his own race. He did just that, winning gold in the event (and for good measure, in the fifteen-hundred, too). He hadn't focused on beating others. He had focused on raising his own peak and becoming as fast as he himself could get. In doing so, he reached the pinnacle of athletic competition.

Cooperation

If competition is our most basic act, cooperation may be our most advanced one. The productive blending of the two is our most ambitious conception, and the most elaborate example is the economic system we depend on: capitalism itself, in which the system works when each individual competes actively, succeeds, and then shares the benefits, creating greater opportunities and new possibilities. So the cycle goes, ideally. The more individuals compete only for themselves and keep the rewards, the less the system succeeds.

Here's a microcosm. You know when you're driving next to a merge lane, and there are those selfish people who, instead of alternating turns with the other cars, decide to race all the way to the front and jump the line? What's the usual outcome? A combination of honks, angry gestures, and stubborn "I'm going to stare straight ahead while not letting you in" looks on the part of those in the primary lane, plus the increasingly bold and hazardous attempts of the selfish person at the front to edge closer and dart in. This one individually competitive move creates a massive and potentially dangerous ripple effect of tense energy and adversarial behavior.

When done right, this "zipper merge" is a wonderful demonstration of urban design, highway engineering and, most of all, cooperative behavior. Each individual driver is competing to achieve their goal of getting to where they're going in the least amount of time possible. And if each of them cooperates with everyone else on the road, the result is collective success, in this case defined by an optimal flow of traffic and everyone reaching their destination as efficiently as possible, with the least amount of mutual stress. All it takes is a single driver to shift from cooperative to selfishly competitive mentality to start the system breaking down.

Some cooperative scenarios work best when everyone in them plays a similar role. When golden eagles hunt, they often work in pairs, one eagle driving the prey to its waiting partner. The roles are interchangeable. What matters is the level of cooperation in pursuit of the larger goal: a meal. Orcas – killer whales (actually a species of dolphin) – hunt in deadly pods of up to forty, working together in highly coordinated attacks to create waves that can knock seals off the ice and into the water, stir up air bubbles to herd schools of fish into a tight ball near the surface, or even take down gray whales by taking turns ramming, biting and pulling on its fins until, after having worn it down, launching from the water onto its blowhole to finish the job.

In other cooperative settings, individuals play different, complementary roles. Lions' collaborative hunting usually involves the males approaching their intended prey upwind, with the intention of driving it towards the lionesses hiding in the bush downwind. After the males have carried out their ambush, the lionesses fan out into a semicircle, into which the prey are herded. Since lions are not as fast as most of their prey, they depend heavily on this cooperation.

There are times when each member of a team aiming for success is an equal link in an interdependent chain, and only by every individual succeeding at their own connected task can the shared goal be achieved. The Ragnar Relay is a multi-person relay race held over two days, one night, and two hundred-ish miles, in which teams of six or twelve individuals pile into a van and take turns running different portions of the overall race. While one person is running, the other members of the team are resting, providing support and encouragement, or driving ahead to meet them at the end of the leg. When the last runner nears the finish, the entire team gathers to cross the tape together and celebrate as one.

The ultimate context of cooperation, the far end of the other side of the spectrum from competition, is a *kibbutz*, a concept originated in Israel in the early twentieth century. Traditionally based in agriculture, a *kibbutz* is a self-contained community in which everyone is an equal contributor, basic living necessities such as food and accommodation are free, and everything is shared. The notion of competition is removed altogether. Today, these collectives have expanded from farming into other areas such as industrial plants and high-tech enterprises, however the principle of total cooperation remains. Whatever needs doing is done by all, and whatever is earned is shared.

Competition and cooperation work equally well, as long as those involved understand and accept which context is at play so that they can perform their best within it. Wolves are impressive examples of both. On one hand, they're superb collaborators, based on the strategic hunting strategies that allow them to take down larger prey – they know instinctively, for example, that the optimal pack size for hunting elk is four, however for a bison, a larger number is needed – along with their highly social ties and their advanced methods of communicating, which include vocalizations, body posture, scent, touch and taste. (Despite popular belief, though wolves howl for many reasons – to assemble the pack, to pass on an alarm, to locate each other during a storm or while crossing unfamiliar territory, and to communicate across great distances – howling at the moon isn't one of them.) They travel in nuclear families, consisting of a mated pair accompanied by their offspring.

On the other hand, competition is just as distinct a part of their nature. Offspring may leave to form their own packs on the onset of sexual maturity and in response to competition for food within the pack. They are territorial; fights within the group are among the principal causes of wolf mortality. And single wolves or mated pairs typically have higher success rates in hunting than do large packs. This is an apex predator into whose fabric competition and cooperation are built equally, each playing important roles in its survival and success.

There are times when what may look like a competitive threat is actually cooperative help. When one gas station opens and starts to draw business, then another one opens across the street, does the second typically put the first out of commission? No – it creates more visibility and volume for both.

Likewise, when multiple flower shops, grocery stores, dentist offices, art galleries, hair salons or vintage clothing outlets appear on one strip or block, is this done on the basis of cutthroat competition, each one aiming to eliminate all the others? No – the idea of doing so is to increase overall demand for that particular type of product or service and a centralized place where people can find it. This is competition and cooperation working together. The cooperation is in the form of sharing space, real estate and customers. The competition is a shared effort to build interest, gain visibility and draw people to the general destination. The result is joint economic benefit.

When Nita and I lived in Georgia, our home sat at the base of a hill, and our kitchen looked out onto a beautiful wooded area in back. One day, while having breakfast, we witnessed a sudden and awesome spectacle: a hawk swooping down from out of nowhere, plucking a squirrel in its talons, and flying away with it behind the house, where there was a treehouse the previous owner had built for his kids. We ran upstairs to our bedroom, both curious. Outside the window, maybe ten feet from our balcony, we watched what felt like a nature program, as though the window were the TV set. After feasting on the squirrel a while, the hawk paused and started calling out in a series of screeches. Was he boasting about his catch? We didn't know; neither of us speaks hawk.

Shortly, the hawk flew off, leaving the unfinished meal. A minute or so later, another hawk arrived, taking the spot of the first, and ate the rest of the dish. Though we never got to ask, we could only assume the two were mates. It was gruesome, riveting, strangely tender, and fully relatable. The most primitive competition of the wild playing itself out right there in front of us, along with, at the very same time, a highly developed act of cooperation, no different than that which we do for each other. (We just use utensils. Most of the time.)

Kaye's Story

After being licensed in real estate for around three months, I was attending a mandatory course. The instructor asked, "What is one of your biggest surprises about the real estate industry?" My answer reflected the most refreshing thing I'd discovered in the industry: that I'd become friends with so many agents from other companies. From the outside, I'd had the impression that it's every man for himself, dog-eat-dog. What I found was that, though we were competitors, it was mutual cooperation that led to collective success.

However, by 2009, the market had shifted, and things had become quite difficult – for me, at least. It seemed others were still managing to do all right despite the tough circumstances. I remember, on one particularly challenging day, observing a friend and fellow agent loading his car with signs for listings he'd just secured. I felt like I was stalled at a certain level, and couldn't break through. My instinctive thought was, he's single, so he has more time to dedicate to the job. I have three children that need my attention. It isn't reasonable to expect that I can pour myself into it the same way, or match that level of success.

At the end of that same day, I was in the office, with my children waiting for me in the breakroom, as was often the case. My realtor friend I'd watched loading the signs was there, too. He adored my kids, and would often take time to sit and chat with them, frequently building them up and encouraging them to work hard and believe in themselves. Despite my jealousy of his success, this endeared me.

Then came a defining moment, and a lesson that permanently changed my outlook. He stopped at my office and started talking to me about my kids, telling me how much he liked them and how impressed he was by them. Misting up a little, he said, "Kaye, you must be doing something right." In that instant, my perspective shifted. I recognized I wasn't competing with him, or anyone else. My purpose was to provide for my family; that's what I was competing for.

That moment happened twelve years ago. Today, my children are wonderful, successful young adults, and I have continued along an upward path and a leadership role. My friend has built a fantastic team and started other businesses. I am happy for his success and proud of the route I have carved. That single lesson changed everything for me: Compete with yourself, cooperate with others.

Chapter 7: Be Appropriately Selfish

In the first six chapters, we've talked exclusively about the things *you* need to do in pursuit of your apex. You yourself, number one, the big cheese. We haven't talked much about others. We will.

In the meantime, you might be saying, *Chad, with all this talk about me – creating the right environment for me, maximizing my strengths, defining my goals, laying out the right path for me – is it all me? Am I meant to pursue my apex in a totally selfish way until I get there?*

No – not in a totally selfish way. Though yes, in a partially selfish way. Maybe selectively or situationally selfish is a better way to say it. We'll get to that in a moment.

When you hear the stories of those who succeed, often you hear that their eyes are always on the ball, they keep their foot on the throttle, they forge ahead with laser focus, letting nothing distract them. Does this mean they're selfish? If we're talking about those who achieve true success, attain the kinds of heights we all aspire to, then yes, they are selfish in the right ways, at appropriate times. In the previous chapter, I discussed the matter of competition versus cooperation, and the circumstances in which you ought to put your head down and focus on your own goals as opposed to those in which it is more sensible, and more advantageous, to work with others around you to accomplish both individual and shared aims.

So are we meant to be selfless all the time, since that's said to be our highest state of being, or should we rather stay focused on what we ourselves need to get done, since that's the best way to ensure success for ourselves and share the benefits with others? Wouldn't it stand to reason that you need to concentrate on yourself to facilitate triumph? Wouldn't every expert tell you that, if you're aiming for a pinnacle, it's practically obligatory to stay zeroed in on it and disregard everything else?

Not exactly. It's a little more nuanced than that. The term "selfish" carries many negative connotations. While the first part of the definition, "seeking or concentrating on one's own advantage, pleasure or well-being," merely sounds like a description of any person's natural state, it's the second part, "without regard for others," that changes the perception.

When you hear about those examples of great success, the people you admire and hold in your esteem and wish to emulate, the behaviors that have gotten them to where they are almost always reflect the first part of the definition (they know what they want, they go after their goals, they maintain untiring focus) and almost never represent the second (they didn't step on the backs of others to get there). They are the right kind of selfish, as a result of which they create success for others as well, they pull people along in their positive wake, and they are celebrated, rather than maligned, for their uncompromising focus and drive. Let's talk about the half a dozen situations in which acting "selfish" is exactly the proper choice:

- ⋏ **When you need to lead others.** Say you're the head of a small business, overseeing a staff of ten. Because you're just starting, there's plenty to do every day, and people are generously wearing multiple hats in the collective effort to achieve escape velocity. For the business to grow, you need to demonstrate strong leadership and clear direction. You need to do this starting with the first moment of every day. You can't achieve the overall goals on your own, and your team can't intuit everything that needs doing. The "selfish" behavior appropriate here is that of taking charge and being the clear alpha, since that's what they need from you to perform successfully, and that's what you owe to them as the person most invested. You must step fully into your role as the captain of the ship, assuming the clear lead and giving precise orders (nicely), which will in fact serve to provide everyone else the ease and assurance that will facilitate their best. If you don't display this "selfishness," it will cause stress and a feeling of aimlessness.

  This kind of leadership can even mean something as simple as choosing the food for lunch when others are waffling. Small acts of decisiveness and direction can have big impacts. Often it's our admirable human instinct to be considerate and say things like, "I'm not sure – which strategy do you think is the more viable one?" In certain situations, this is right. It contributes to a feeling of team, it gives different people a voice, and it invites different insights and perspectives. However, if what is needed is a leader, and if that leader is clearly you, then lead. Others will be grateful to you for this selfishness, and they will deliver results because of it.

▲ **When you need to learn something new**. As the famous comedian Jerry Lewis said, "You can't be faulted for being selfish if you're going to get better because of it." Maybe you're putting your head down for six weeks to get trained in a new skill that will make you a more valuable asset to your team afterwards. Perhaps you've been granted approval to do a graduate degree concurrently with your job, which entails working during the day and studying during evenings and weekends for six months, so you're essentially going to be a hermit for that period, for the benefit of coming out the other side with that diploma and new knowledge. Maybe you've pledged to get in better shape and therefore have told your family that, for the next eight weeks, your hour from five to six p.m. every single day will be dedicated to exercising, inviolably and without interruption, except for emergencies. All of these behaviors, which may look selfish on the surface, both contribute to your own betterment and serve to benefit those around you.

This positive selfishness is instinctive in the first days of all mammals, even those destined to eventually rule their environments. Polar bear cubs are born blind, toothless and covered in a sparse layer of soft, short fur. These newborns are only about twenty-five centimeters long and weigh around one kilogram before they start growing rapidly thanks to their mother's rich milk. The cubs have no choice – they need to be selfish, for it's her milk only that will allow them to grow, and it's in that period specifically that they require it. This selfishness, born of vulnerability, allows them to obtain the nutrients that will turn them into the apex hunters they need to be to survive.

▲ **When you're intentionally laying low.** Ever seen a snow leopard outside of *National Geographic* or the zoo? Me, neither. There are reasons. First, these exquisite animals are notorious for their shy demeanor. Second, they are crepuscular animals – active mostly at dawn and dusk. And most significant, they are solitary creatures who deliberately maintain distance from others of the same species. Carving out their own range in this way – they usually keep a distance of at least a mile between themselves and other members – confers a number of benefits, not least of which is domain over the prey within that area, which can include animals three times the weight of the leopard, such as sheep, ibex and deer. Sure, hanging out with other snow leopards might be fun, however this selfishness is essential for each individual, and therefore the species, to thrive.

You may be doing much the same, for the purpose of carving out your own space. Perhaps you're developing a new innovation you need to keep secret, for now. Maybe you need a little self-imposed isolation to finish an important project. Could be you're devoting all your time and energy to analyzing a certain portion of the market where you feel you can make a successful entry if you time it just right. There is absolutely a time to display this kind of selfishness, and others will respect and understand it, because they've no doubt had the need to do the same.

⋏ **When you're seizing the day.** The world teaches us to be kind, to share, to act altruistically, to show empathy, and to think about what it feels like to be in others' shoes. These are all good things to be, and do – however they need to be balanced by the ability to recognize when you ought to be fighting for yourself and asserting your own selfish needs. There's nothing wrong with drive, desire, ambition, and aiming for the top of the food chain. Putting others first has to be defined properly and done in the right contexts, at the right time, for the right reasons, not done indiscriminately and with the outcome of you finding yourself behind, on the outside looking in, or watching someone else glory in the achievement that should have rightfully been yours. The saying "Nice guys finish last" isn't true, because being nice is never a disadvantage, however it is true that "Nice guys who don't act in their own selfish interest when it is right to do so often regret not having done so because then they don't end up accomplishing what they had every right to."

In this way, being selfish simply equates to taking control of your own fate and seizing the opportunities you've prepared for. This is not about acting in the wrong way toward others or getting them to fall in line with your goals. This is about you fighting for you, advocating for your needs, and reaping the rewards you deserve. Oscar Wilde said, "A red rose is not selfish because it wants to be a red rose. It would be horribly selfish if it wanted all the other flowers in the garden to be both red and roses." Be the red rose you are, and do the things you need to do to blossom.

⋏ **When you're engaging in R&R.** That is, rest and recovery. Replenishment. Recharging. Renewal. We all need it, and we all end up better for it. This kind of "selfishness" might be better termed "self-care." There is a reason why, when you're in an airplane watching the safety demonstration, you're told to put the oxygen mask on yourself first before putting it on your children, because if you're passed out, you're not going to be much help to them. I've often heard this spoken about through the analogy of one's glass being full or empty. If my glass is empty, I can't help fill yours. If mine is full, I have the energy and nourishment I need to do what I need to do to ensure your success.

This applies to all of our pursuits, including work, family, and every other facet of life. Only by ensuring that you're on firm ground yourself can you be your best for your colleagues, your partner, your family, your friends. If you don't act selfishly by taking the moments you need to make sure you're sound and stable, what you bring to others will be less than your best self.

It's easy to forget this, or ignore it. We often operate from a mode of self-sacrifice. For our children, we give up our food, our money and our sleep. These are all part of the natural state of parenting, however if we do these selfless things to the point of breaking down, the people we're intending to take care of in fact suffer. Being selfish about your own wellness and grounding helps them much more than if you never pay attention to your own needs. Every relationship requires a healthy balance of selflessness versus selfishness, or, more simply, give versus take. How many marriages fail when the kids go off to school or move out because the couple that was once in love put aside their own needs and desires to such an extent that they were never able to retrieve what they had? It isn't their fault – they just made the accidental and fatal mistake of never being selfish about their relationship, and ended up so far apart as a result that the gulf was too big to repair.

My first marriage is an unfortunate example of this. Things were good before we had a child. I fell in love with this child and always put her first, forgetting to act selfish about my relationship with my now ex-wife in parallel. At the same time, my now ex-wife did honor her own needs, putting herself first, focusing on getting back into shape, and selfishly pursuing some of the fun she felt she'd missed during pregnancy. The imbalance pushed us apart, so much so that we split before our daughter even started school. At the time, I didn't have the wisdom to understand it. Thankfully, the lessons I learned then help me – I hope – be a better partner today. As bestselling author and strategist Richie Norton puts it, "Selfishness at the expense of others is bad. Self-care for the betterment of others is good."

▲ **When you need support.** Asking for help is one of our most difficult acts in life. To do so feels selfish, embarrassing, awkward, weak, desperate, imposing, presumptuous…the list goes on. Most of us hate the mere idea of it. Yet, of all the selfish acts, it's perhaps the most important and most beneficial to you and those around you.

These "selfish" reach-outs can be small – you have a barrier at work that only your supervisor can remove. They can be big – you need someone to watch your dog for the week because one of your parents is sick and you need to go out of town to be with them. They can be intangible – you need a pep talk or a stern lecture. They can be material – you need to borrow a cup of sugar, or a pair of gloves, or a hundred bucks. Whenever you feel that asking for help would be selfish, ask yourself this: How would you feel if you knew that someone you cared about could have used your help yet chose not to ask for it? Seeking the support of others is the most unselfish "selfish" behavior in our wide repertoire. It takes courage, vulnerability and self-awareness, and it will always be met with a positive response.

A study done at Yale provided evidence that humans aren't hardwired to be selfish in the extreme or universally cooperative, either. We naturally toggle back and forth, depending on the situation and the circumstances. You might see this as counterintuitive, thinking that in our ancestry we needed to be tremendously selfish to survive and that today we get ahead only by cooperating and being selfless.

Neither is true. To keep striding forward, our ancestors needed to balance selflessness and selfishness just as much as we do. If any of them had been all of one or all of the other, they'd have run into the same problems we would. (Their problems would just have longer, curved teeth.) What's the right relative weight between acting selfless or selfish? It can be elusive, both in individual moments and in the big picture. The proportion is different for everyone, since no two lives are the same and we all are seeking different goals, in different settings and environments, at various points, and with separate sets of skills, abilities and supports. Seek your optimum balance of these two necessary and natural traits as you pursue your apex, always keeping in mind that, to reach it, there are times when being "selfish" is precisely what you ought to be.

Phyllis's Story

I've worked in health care for nearly half a century – as a nurse for forty-three years, and also as a professional coach for health care workers for the past twenty. In other words, one part of my job is taking care of patients directly, and the other part is taking care of others who take care of patients, as well as their families.

In our field today, there's a serious risk of what we call caregiver fatigue. It involves a clash between the need to deliver service as a business and the desire to provide care in a genuine way. In recent decades, the training of health care professionals has involved endless messaging about things like making evidence-based decisions, getting published in academic journals, doing clinical research, and getting multiple certifications. In this way, it's evolved into a highly transactional atmosphere. Patients today are better informed, and they have higher expectations. However, most health care organizations and venues are run by accounting and finance people, as opposed to those who actually practice and know what it feels like. So you've got this internal contradiction: the people running things remain focused on the transaction, while patients expect a sincere human experience.

Hence the conflict felt by so many in the field. Health care executives ask me why they need someone to, for example, help nurses become more compassionate. "Aren't they naturally compassionate?" they ask me. I tell them, yes, of course they are, however they're being told to render care "slicker and quicker" – meaning hit monetary targets, focus on the bottom line. They're being asked to think like cold businesspeople rather than health care providers. All of it stands in contrast to the reason most of us got into this field in the first place.

That gets back to the growing trend of caregiver burnout and psychological stress. Virtually anyone you find in this field has chosen it as a calling. Now they face this gap between what they're being asked to focus on from a business lens and what they feel the job should be about. So the question is, how do you close that gap? How do you feed your family and still nourish your soul?

The key part of the answer is self-care. It's crucial today to teach people what it is and how to do it. Looking after oneself has become a vital skill, from the mailroom to the C-suite. It isn't always easy, especially for those who have chosen a profession dedicated to caring for others. That's where I offer help.

The process is about self-awareness and self-examination – the two sides of the self-care coin. Having the strength and courage to work with yourself, to be curious about yourself, helps put the why back into what we do, as opposed to just the what that we're asked to manage. As I said, it can feel counter-instinctive for healthcare professionals to make themselves a priority.

My goal is to help them understand that working on yourself allows you to be a better caregiver to others. It isn't selfish work; quite the contrary, as a matter of fact. There are some situations you can't change, and you need to understand how to work through those. There are triggers and biases that are different for everyone, and it helps to become aware of those. There are self-sabotaging behaviors we all engage in, and it's crucial to recognize why and when they happen so that we can avoid their depleting us. All of these things contribute to being able to remain your real self even in an environment where you're being asked to be something different.

When you do the process well, that close encounter with yourself doesn't cause you to shut down (or toughen up, which is what we're often advised to do). Rather, it allows you to better understand yourself and reconcile that transactional-versus-transformational conflict, making the job feel more like those we envisioned when we entered the field: part of a partnership of caregiving and receiving, based on empathy and compassion. It connects you back to your original mission, that purpose that drew you to the field in the first place. Once you make that breakthrough, it strengthens every moment in which you render care. Working on yourself isn't selfish. It benefits you, and everyone you come in contact with.

Chapter 8: Make *Real*ationships

Mark Messier is one of the most applauded and respected leaders in the annals of sport. He played for a staggering twenty-five years in the National Hockey League and is the only player in the league's history to captain two different championship teams. During the 1994 playoffs, playing for a New York Rangers team that hadn't won a title in fifty-four years and was facing elimination, Messier made his most famous literal and symbolic statement when he told the media, "I guarantee we'll win tonight," then put the team on his back by scoring three goals in that game and ultimately leading his team to its first Stanley Cup in over half a century. Known for his mix of skill and grit, his perseverance, and his ability to raise the play of others around him, he'd been nicknamed both "The Moose" and "The Messiah."

In 2021, seventeen years after retiring from the game, Messier released a memoir. What was the title of the memoir by this great individual leader and one of the most accomplished performers of all time in his sport? *No One Wins Alone.*

Likes, Followers, Influences and Connections

Messier is right: no one reaches great heights in a vacuum. Make no mistake, each of us is answerable for our behaviors, responsible for the steps we take or don't, and accountable to every decision, action and response in our lives. However, true success doesn't result from the efforts of one person in isolation, and consistent achievement isn't the outcome of individual struggle and determination independent of others. While what you do individually has weight and consequence, equally powerful are the connections you have with others, and the way those relationships affect your journey toward the summits you strive for.

In 2017, rock climber Alex Honnold became the first human to "free-solo" (climb unaided by ropes or any other gear) the three-thousand-foot sheer rock face of El Capitan in Yosemite National Park. Though to the eyes of the world, this physical feat was performed alone, in truth it represented a remarkable step forward in a cumulative journey taken by many others since the popularization of climbing in the 1950s, when a small group of like-minded spirits found their way to Yosemite and began navigating their way up its immense walls.

This first band of climbers, and hundreds of others in the decades that followed, made attempts, charted routes, modified styles and approaches, sometimes succeeded, often failed, and added one new achievement after another, providing the ongoing foundation for Honnold's "solo" exploit. This stunning feat, an individual one to our perception, was set in motion decades earlier by the collective drive, focus and camaraderie of an unknown number of others devoted to similar goals and to pursuing, in this case quite literally, a common apex.

In this, the age of social media, where "likes" are the most sought-after currency, "followers" are the most valued stamp of influence, and the most essential type of communication is amount of "content," how many people that you're connected to – be honest now – do you really know? How many would you say you have a relationship with? How many of them have you met? How many could you even recognize walking down the street? Of all these connections, how many would you tell me are genuine?

In short, how many of your relationships are *real*ationships?

The Real in *Real*ationships

*Real*ationships are those with people who know you. Really know you. They can describe what you do for work, life and play. They know what you stand for and believe in. They're familiar with what excites you and what ticks you off.

*Real*ationships are those with people who can predict what you'd do in a situation and how you'd react to a challenge. They're the people you depend on to encourage you to be your best, to call you out when you're being less than that, and who know they can say anything to you without fear of repercussions. They're the ones who call you for help anytime, are present in good moments and bad, and acknowledge your most impressive feats and most foolish acts with the same candidness.

*Real*ationships are those with people who you want to tell good news to, celebrate important occasions with, and bounce ideas off of. They are rich, intimate associations characterized by depth, caring, reciprocity and true closeness.

The value of *real*ationships is challenged today, when we're constantly and irrationally pressured to feel that the quantity of our connections is more valuable than their quality. Your number of Facebook friends, Instagram followers or LinkedIn connections may feel like they give you cachet and significance. In real terms, what is the nature of each of these connections? How do you feel about them, and what effect do they have on your daily life, your motivation, your growth, your sense of self?

When you establish, maintain and invest in *real*ationships, you see the rewards. I'm not talking about material rewards; that isn't the aim of sincere connections. I mean that the people in your life with whom you have the truest relationships are the ones who provide the truest value. They support you in your pursuits; they act as a safety net when you falter; they push you to keep exploring your boundaries; and they act as a sounding board for your most promising ideas and wildest flights of fancy. The *real*ationships in your life are the ones that both keep you grounded and give you wings. You know who these people are. You instinctively turn to them to talk to, to listen, to vent, to give advice, to consider, to debate, and to confess. And they come to you just as often, for the same reasons.

A caveat: I'm not saying social media and *real*ationships are mutually exclusive. Today's technology is a godsend for staying in touch with people in different places, watching their families grow, feeling connected to the important moments in their lives, and being there for them, even if only virtually. Just today I met a woman who tomorrow will see her sister for the first time after she immigrated to North America from the Middle East ten years ago. At first, the two had to correspond by sending faxes. Soon, the magic of smartphones and apps like FaceTime made it possible for them to speak every day, see each other's faces, hear each other's voices, and develop relationships with each other's kids, until this magical day when they will finally reunite. If that isn't a testimony for the unique power of social media, I don't know what is.

What I am saying is there is a tendency in today's world for people to conduct their relationships so obsessively via social media that they lose sight of what counts as a *real*ationship. Heck, one of the very definitions of the word "real" is "existing or occurring in the physical world." Do you maintain most of your relationships in the real, physical world, or the removed, online one?

You see it in business, too. Watch someone at a random networking event you'll probably observe them flitting about the room in an attempt to interact with as many others as possible and come away with as big a list of contacts as they can. Anyone can attend a business function and meet new people, or fill a database with names. Most people who attend these events, seeking to connect briefly with everyone in the room because you never know who the "right" person is, come away from it having met everyone yet having built a connection with no one. And the usual result of all this frenetic effort is that all of the calls that person will make within the next few days will be ignored or amount to nothing because a genuine foundation was never laid.

How many *real*ationships can we have? How many is it reasonable to maintain? Don't put a limit on it. Experts discuss this frequently, some saying we can have only a handful, others saying up to a hundred, since our earliest ancestral tribes were made up of approximately that many. Don't think about it as a quota you should meet. Let it be organic. We're each individual in our makeup. It may be natural for you to forge true connections with a wide circle of people, whereas for someone else, the right number may be much lower, yet still provide the same overall value. Think more about the importance of applying the principles of *real*ationships than hitting a minimum number. (That's social media mentality sneaking in again.)

So how do you create *real*ationships? Sure, there are the built-in connections you may already have – your close friends from high school who would give you the shirt off their back, the colleagues at work with whom you've become tight, your childhood best friend who lives across the country, with whom you don't miss a beat whenever you see each other, your parents and siblings, who would give their lives before yours. What about others? How do you continue to sow genuine connections in a world that moves so fast and pulls you in so many directions? Let me suggest five simple and powerful ways:

- ▲ Be present. Bring your authentic self to every moment you can. When you interact with another person, demonstrate your attention. Lift your head up from your phone. Listen actively. Transmit positive energy. Absorb what they're saying. Ask questions (using the FORD categories, for example: Family,

Occupation, Recreation, Dreams). Show interest. Respond meaningfully.

▲ Make no assumptions or predictions about others when you first meet them. It takes time to really get to know someone. Don't make snap judgments during a first interaction or start making private guesses about where in the constellation of your relationships this individual could fit, or to what end. I have a colleague who refers to the relationship "chessboard," meaning there are countless unforeseeable ways in which one connection may lead to others, and you never know which relationships – or when, or under what circumstances – may become something you couldn't have envisioned. She and her husband started out owning a small video production company. A while back, hoping to expand, they made lots of cold calls, getting just one reply. Bringing their best to that one connection, they won the business and established a genuine relationship with the main contact at their new client. When, a year later, that person left the company, they had no idea where she'd gone, until a few months after, they received a call from her saying she'd moved to a company further south. They got the exclusive contract to shoot videos for the person's new company. A year after that, they were looking for a partner to launch a new technology for the business, and ended up finding someone ideal based on referrals from those with whom they'd forged strong relationships at the new client's. Eighteen months after that, the business now having grown, they were seeking someone to help run things, and found the right candidate through a connection from the person who had become the technology partner. This individual was reluctant to meet at first because he'd been with his current company for a long time and felt comfortable. He eventually agreed to an initial chat based on the strength and sincerity of the referrals, and after more dialogue, accepted the position. Today, my colleague and her husband have a thriving business and a chessboard filled with *real*ationships, all connected to one another.

▲ Remove all expectations. Think about who the other person is rather than how the relationship might benefit you. Give to give, not to get.

▲ Treat everyone with respect, dignity and kindness, always.

▲ As often as possible, let others see your best you.

What might change if the same people who attend those networking events intending to collect as many names and numbers as possible were instead to go in with the intention of making real connections, based on the five principles above? Some years back, a friend of mine was attending an industry event and found himself compelled by the keynote speaker. It wasn't because the person seemed like he could be instrumental in my friend's career or help him achieve specific goals. It was because this individual's speech resonated with my friend, who was at an important crossroads in his life.

At that event, there was no opportunity for my friend to meet the speaker, since the crowd was huge and the gentleman was ushered out immediately after his speech. A couple of years later, my friend was attending a different event, smaller this time, and that same person turned out to be the keynote speaker. With encouragement from his wife, my friend mustered the courage to walk up, introduce himself, and let the speaker know how much the message had struck him, and how he'd been applying the lessons in his own life and had already felt a change.

After the event, my friend looked up the speaker (who lived in a different city) on Facebook and developed the connection through polite correspondence and messages that were honest, relevant and real. Eventually the two connected by phone. That first brief call became a longer one a few weeks later. That longer call turned into regular communication, then an informal mentorship, then a unique and sustained *real*ationship, based on truth, trust and transparency, which continues today.

Jim's Story

Every success I've had, and every step up the ladder, has been due to making real and authentic relationships. I got my first job teaching at an exclusive private school because of a relationship I had being a counselor at camp. I landed my first opportunity in real estate because of my relationship from the private school. I then got a job at a boutique high-end firm because of a relationship at a men's bible study group.

I never went into any of those places thinking, this will be a great place to network for a future job. Instead, I entered each situation fully present and ready to give of myself. It wasn't a matter of what I could expect in return. When you do that, you don't bring your authentic self to any interaction; you're just thinking about the transaction that might result. I came to every new position with honor, never intentionally burned bridges, and always upheld the personal goal of simply doing my best. I call it an attitude of gratitude, as opposed to a "What can you do for me?" mentality, which I feel predisposes you in the wrong way from the start.

When I say coming to every situation with honor, what I mean is building trust in a sincere, not phony, way. If you can go into a relationship with no agenda, it allows other people to be their real selves with you just as you're being your real self with them. Coming in with honor means that instead of guiding the interaction toward a predetermined goal in your head, you let it develop naturally and organically, allowing for a mutual determination of what's best. If you're always thinking you need to win at the expense of the other person losing, you will ultimately fail. I've found that adopting a win-win approach from the start leads to greater success. If you begin by asking what can benefit both parties, then it becomes simply a matter of setting clear expectations and having open communication.

Maintaining true relationships includes acknowledging one's mistakes. I've certainly made my share of them. They happened, and I know that I need to own them in order to continue being my best self. For example, a friend once generously gave me tickets to a sporting event, and I said I'd pay him back. For some reason, time passed and I never reimbursed him for the tickets. When I saw him a year or so later, he didn't bring it up. It always nagged at me that I didn't do what I said I would. His graciousness taught me a lesson about forgiveness, though I was still disappointed in myself.

That's just one of many mistakes I've made. I'm grateful that, in all of these cases, the people I didn't treat as well as I should have exhibited grace and compassion toward me, just like my friend with the tickets. Seeing others model this kind of grace and integrity reinforced in me the belief that there is no other way to be. I've learned both parts of the lesson over and over in my career and in my life. First, be your real self with others and treat them with respect. Second, be willing to give them grace when they make a mistake and hopefully they will do the same for you.

Today I am still in a position of leadership, and I demonstrate these lessons as much as I can. My greatest passion is sharing the importance of great relationships and modeling them every day.

Chapter 9: Embrace Obstacles

The hundred-meter hurdles has always been something of a curiosity to me. The hundred-meter dash, I get – it's natural for us to want to know how fast we can run in a straight line over a specific distance. Of all track and field titles, there is none more glamorous than fastest human.

I've forever wondered, though, what instinct led to the addition of a series of standing barriers to create a new version of the race, in 1896, the first modern Olympics. Perhaps one of the committee members, watching the hundred-meter sprinters practice, said to another, "I have an idea – why don't we create a new event similar to this one, except with a bunch of wooden hurdles they have to jump over every ten meters in a totally unnatural and potentially hazardous way?" Then a third said, "That's a terrific idea, I don't know why we didn't think of it before. I'll do you one better – I hear they do this race in the UK that's three thousand meters and has a bunch of those hurdles, including one thick one that has a water pit on the other side of it. Steeple-something. Now *that* would be fun to watch."

Okay, that may not be an exact version of what happened. My point is the inclination to challenge ourselves is so ingrained that we don't merely anticipate obstacles – we even create them where they don't need to exist.

This is an admirable and, evolutionarily speaking, necessary trait. We test ourselves constantly with challenges that are in our control so that we can hopefully better meet the challenges we can't predict. You probably do this much more than you think, because the ways in which you do it are subtle and you don't likely see them as self-tests while you're doing them. You absently pick up a couple of balls to see if you can juggle them. You delay scratching an itch to see how long you can hold out. You force yourself to ask someone on a date even though you're shaking in your boots. You resist ordering the brownie sundae. We create these tests for ourselves, both physical and mental, all the time, rarely conscious of why we're doing so.

Heck, look at a bunch of school kids playing Red Rover, a game in which two lines of kids hold hands or link arms and take turns calling individuals from the line on the opposite side to run at them and attempt to break one of the links in the human chain. The game might look positively barbaric to an uninformed observer, since the only guideline is, "I'm going to run at you as violently as I can and you're going to do your best to stop me." Though it looks fun on the surface (and it is), clearly there is a deeper driving force: our instinct to put barriers in our own way and see if we can conquer them.

Do you know the similar schoolyard game called British Bulldog? It's a bigger, wilder version of Red Rover, in which kids line up on one side of a field and another group of kids designated as the "bulldogs" stand in the middle of the field and, once the others start running, do all they can to "capture" them before they reach the other side. Anyone caught by the bulldogs then becomes a bulldog, so each round becomes more ferocious and intense until there is only one survivor…ahem, winner. Talk about the instinct for putting obstacles in our own way! This one is so primitive, it's been banned from many schools.

Do you know why we're ticklish? No one else does, either. Psychologists, biologists and even philosophers dating back to Plato and Darwin have offered theories, yet no one has ever figured out the reason for this reflex we all share. One hypothesis is that it's a kind of built-in obstacle, an automatic defense mechanism that encourages the development of combat skills through the non-threatening version of it done by parents, siblings and friends. Since we generally make movements to get away, we also laugh, encouraging it. Given this natural cue to continue, suggests the theory, there must be an intrinsic reason for it.

Yes, we test ourselves, instinctively, unconsciously, and even in ways our greatest thinkers can't figure out. The only thing we seem to know is that it's essential for us to embrace these tests, because doing so makes us better, stronger, more capable versions of ourselves.

The Buffer Zone

Some time back, a colleague gave me a piece of advice I've never forgotten. "The best way to manage obstacles," he said, "is by minimizing the likelihood of them coming up in the first place, at least as much as it's possible."

The example he used was preparing for a meeting. "Say you're giving a presentation tomorrow morning at ten and everyone needs a printed version of it," he said. "When would you ordinarily print the materials?"

I proudly replied, "I'd get up early and do the printing right away so they're ready well before the meeting."

"Okay," he said. "And what will you do if the printer is out of toner? Do you know how to change it? Do you know where the toner is? Do you know who to call if you can't find it? Do you know how long it takes to change? What if there's an issue with your computer and you can't send the file to the printer? Do you know how to troubleshoot every possible computer problem that might arise, within the hour or two buffer time you're allowing yourself? What if you suddenly notice an error on one page that has implications for several others? Will you have enough time to fix the whole presentation and still print all of the copies in time for the meeting?"

I was silent. I'd gotten the point. He made it explicit anyway.

"By waiting until the last few hours, you're creating – to be honest, inviting – a higher possibility of snags and snafus than necessary. You can't control things one hundred percent. Why not control them as much as possible by providing yourself a reasonable buffer?"

I asked him how much was reasonable.

"Two days minimum. If the meeting is Friday morning, have everything ready Wednesday. Problems take time to fix. Why cause yourself, and maybe others, undue stress? Why have so many scenarios that could result in you not being ready in time and able to deliver the way you know you can? Why allow any more potential than necessary for an unseen obstacle to prevent you from succeeding? Control the things you can and prepare for the things you can't."

Ever since that day, whenever I have something I need to prepare, or a deadline to meet, or a deliverable to deliver, I take the original date and move it up at least two days. There have been many occasions where an unforeseen issue has come up and, because I've built in that extra cushion, I've been able to rectify it and still meet the intended timeline with the minimum amount of stress or scrambling. In Steven Covey's renowned *The Seven Habits of Highly Effective People*, habit number one is "Be proactive, not reactive."

Be prepared for hitches and hurdles. Anticipate what could go wrong and mitigate those possibilities ahead of time instead of having to react in the moment without the proper means, whether practical or emotional.

Though you can't prevent obstacles from showing up, you can create the highest possibility of managing them.

Rope Climbs, Best Fit Lines and a Mythical Channel

Large obstacles sometimes require small fixes. Likewise, small ones sometimes demand elaborate solutions. No two hurdles are the same (except the ones in an actual hurdle race, which are exactly the same), nor are any two people the same. When you encounter a barrier, you will confront it in a way that is uniquely you, though often you'll do it with the help of others.

A while back, a group of friends got me into obstacle course races, and I've since participated in a number of different types, including Spartan races – a series of races containing multiple obstacles of varying difficulty over a range of distances. One of the staple obstacles in these races is a twenty-foot rope-climb after which one must hit the bell after reaching the top. The first several times I tried it, I'd get just one or two pulls up the rope before failing, which meant having to do thirty burpees (and if you've ever done thirty burpees in the middle of a race, you understand why failing an obstacle is seriously undesirable).

Obsessed with this obstacle, I finished work one day and, still in my suit, walked into a CrossFit-style gym saying I was looking for a place where I could learn how to climb a rope. The manager introduced himself and said "I bet I can teach you how to do that in thirty seconds – in that outfit."

Despite his boast, I changed into gym clothes. He taught me a certain strategy with specific techniques and mechanics. I still couldn't get it and reached no higher than I had before, during the races. Then one of the coaches in the gym saw me struggling and took me aside, saying the manager's approach works for some and not others. He offered to teach me using a different method, which involved the simplest possible modification: switching from an outside leg hook to an inside one. I got to the top in thirty seconds and since that day have never failed at the rope climb.

Whether it's finding a way around a fallen branch in the road, conquering a rope ascent, managing significant family issues, curing major diseases, or all points in between, the obstacles in our lives gratefully come in all types and sizes, and they don't discriminate from one person to another. I say gratefully because in each of these challenges is contained the opportunity for growth and self-improvement. We all face them, and none of us knows which ones will arise when. The only common thread is that when they do crop up, we are forced to do something about them, and because of that, we discover things about our own capabilities that we don't find out when things are easy.

Do you know anyone who would say that they've so far had a life unimpeded by any sudden bumps in the road or unexpected twists in the journey? Neither do I. Those bumps and twists are what make life real. They test us, regularly, spontaneously and unpredictably, and as a result, let us know that we can handle the unexpected and still forge ahead. The path to your apex is never going to be straight and predictable. That would be too boring, and too easy. Without having to face challenges along our path, we'd never have the opportunity to change or evolve. We'd never know what we can handle, or what we're made of.

Are you familiar with the math concept called the "best fit line"? (Math is not one of my strong suits, so I'm going to take this slowly, for my own sake.) When you have a chart with two axes and a bunch of different individually scattered data points, the best fit line is the most direct path through the average they collectively form.

When pursuing a goal, there is your starting point and your aimed-for end point. When you eventually reach it, and you look back to see how you got there, you'll never witness a direct route; you'll see lots of zigs and zags, stops and starts, hits and misses. You'll appreciate the complications and impediments that inevitably arose, along with the ways in which you figured out how to get around, over or through them. You'll have traveled your best fit line to keep moving forward and upward, to reach that peak.

One of the most ambitious examples of confronting obstacles in human history is the search for the famed Northwest Passage – a shorter route from the Atlantic Ocean to the Pacific across the Arctic Archipelago – starting in the fifteenth century. This elusive route from Europe to East Asia was envisioned as early as the second century A.D. by the great Greco-Roman astronomer and geographer Ptolemy, and first explored in 1497 by John Cabot, a Venetian living in England. Making landfall in the Canadian Maritimes (there I go using another excuse to mention Canada),

Cabot, like Christopher Columbus five years earlier, thought he had reached the shores of Asia, achieving the landmark feat. Instead, he soon realized his blunder, returned home, and later set out again for the legendary route, only to disappear forever.

Over the next four centuries, many other adventurers and would-be opportunists discovered just how formidable a barrier this mythical passage was. Jacques Cartier made three separate voyages from France, reached as far as Quebec, dealt with scurvy and angry Iroquois, and retired to a quiet town in Brittany. The Spaniard Francisco de Ulloa set sail from Acapulco in 1539 and got to the Gulf of California before abruptly turning back. Englishman Henry Hudson, hired by the Dutch East India Company, embarked early in the seventeenth century, sailed around Long Island into what is now the Hudson River, returned home, tried again a year later, and got stuck within the massive body of water now called Hudson's Bay (no coincidence that he ended up in two different water bodies bearing his name), where he drifted for months before becoming trapped by ice. The following spring, his crew mutinied, setting Hudson adrift in a small boat and turning back for England. He was never seen again. And there is the infamous and tragic Franklin Expedition of 1845, in which two ships vanished along with their one hundred twenty-eight crew, some of whose skeletons would be discovered a century and a half later by archaeologists in the Canadian Arctic.

It would not be until 1850 that Irishman Robert McClure and his crew confirmed the existence of the Northwest Passage, traversing the water via ship and the ice via sled, and not until 1906 that Norwegian explorer Roald Amundsen made the entire passage by sea, reaching the coast of Alaska. Today, due to climate change, the route is open and free of ice. In 2010, two gray whales, native to the Pacific Ocean, were spotted in the Atlantic for the first time in over two hundred years, possibly having made passage through the newly open waters.

Why the long history lesson on the Northwest Passage? As a reminder, and a celebration – of the ways we naturally invite obstacles to test us, of the resilience we possess in confronting and conquering them, and of the amazing things we can accomplish as a result.

Nick's Story

We were living a very pleasant, blessed life here in Charlotte, North Carolina, when, just after the start of the New Year, and a week before my son's eighth birthday, my wife was diagnosed with breast cancer. A few weeks later, she had to go under the knife. Complications during surgery caused her to need a chest tube and to have to stay in the hospital for an extra week, which included Valentine's Day. Then came the news that she would need chemotherapy. Not what one would call a great start to the year.

In March, the hits kept on coming with the arrival of Covid-19, which meant I was no longer allowed to accompany her. For the next several months, we continued that way – me dropping her at the hospital and her having to undergo the chemo on her own. At the same time, we were home-schooling our kids, in kindergarten and second grade, respectively, and pivoting in almost every other area of our lives as well. Our world, like everyone else's, had quickly been turned upside down.

Amid this chaos and difficulty, it would have been the easiest thing in the world to fall into a negative spiral. Instead, we made a conscious decision to focus on the things we could control. We had no say in my wife's diagnosis. We had no influence over the pandemic. These were nature's decisions.

One of the side effects of chemo is, of course, hair loss. That was something else over which we had no control. So we decided that, though we may not be able to prevent her losing her hair, we did have the ability to decide when. My wife and I agreed to both shave our heads, at the same time. I shaved hers, and she shaved mine. My eight-year-old son and six-year-old daughter said they wanted to be part of it, too. I was so proud of them, and so moved. We didn't want to shave their entire heads, so we did just a strip on the side, for the symbolic gesture.

Our doing this as a unit gave my wife back a feeling of power over this scary and unpredictable thing. Everyone in the family looks back on that night as a memorable experience, and a pivotal moment in which we used our shared strength to change what could have been a very dark period into something unforgettable, even beautiful. It helped shift our mindset about the whole experience. It showed her, and us, how we could rally against the fear as an unbreakable team.

To combat the multilayered challenges produced by Covid – from the practical and logistical to the emotional and psychological – we did another, similar, thing. Rather than give in to the frustration it was causing, we embedded a daily ritual that, though it sounds simple, proved quite powerful: having dinner together. Again, we knew we couldn't directly influence most of what was going on around us, so we made a pact to do this small act each night as a way to stay connected amid all the external chaos, and to remind ourselves that, despite this unprecedented time of challenge, there was a lot to be thankful for. We would go around the table and name something we were grateful for that day. It didn't have to be big or momentous; it was more about the ritual. As I said, though it may seem like a small, simple thing, it soon became our shared mantra. It helped instill in our kids a mindset of gratitude, and it helped give us an even greater shared feeling of control and positivity.

The dinner ritual became so meaningful to us that we soon added exercise to the nightly routine. For about six months before the start of the pandemic, my kids and I had been training in Brazilian jiu-jitsu at a nearby gym. Since we'd of course had to stop doing that, we replaced it with exercising together as a family on most nights. Just twenty or thirty minutes to do something physical – pushups, situps, anything. Again, the type of exercise mattered less than the custom itself, and the feeling it gave us. Most of life isn't predictable, though one thing is: you're going to face some hurdles along the way. By focusing on the things you can control, and giving thanks for the small stuff, you can manage the rest.

Chapter 10: Adapt

If anything characterizes us as humans, it's our ability to adapt. As far as evolution goes, it may be our most impressive ongoing feat. Since our early ancestors took the stage about a hundred thousand years ago, we've continued to change according to the different environments we've experienced, becoming generally shorter, lighter and smaller-boned.

We've also dispersed across the globe, resulting in a profusion of adaptations and producing the wonderful diversity we see today. Our bodies have become shorter and stockier in colder climates and longer and leaner in warm ones. Those in regions of extreme cold have extra fat on their faces for additional warmth, while those in regions of extreme warmth have larger, thicker lips to help evaporate moisture and cool the body. People in colder climates more often have straight hair to keep the head and neck warm and let cold moisture run off the scalp more easily, whereas those in warmer environments are more likely to have tight, curly hair to keep more of the neck and scalp exposed and better facilitate cooling and evaporation of sweat.

These adaptations can be phenomenally specific. Hot, humid climates have produced humans with flatter, broader noses that allow inhaled air to be better moistened and retained; hot, dry climates have created those with narrowed, projecting noses that reduce the amount of water lost from the lungs during breathing; and cold, dry climates have led to populations with smaller, longer and narrower noses to moisten and warm incoming air. Northern and East Asian populations have a distinctive fold of skin that protects their eyes from hard-driving storms and snow glare. Australian Aboriginals of the Central Desert, whose climate can be freezing for short periods, have evolved the ability to drop their bodies to lower temperatures without triggering the usual shiver reflex (whereas I make a beeline for the thermostat at the first sign of cold weather).

It is by the luck of the draw that, from a still unknown tangle of evolutionary branches, our descendants passed on adaptations to our surroundings that gave us an edge, and that these beneficial traits were passed on through the eons until, from the several human species who walked the Earth several million years ago, only *Homo sapiens* emerged. It's this continuing magic trick more than any other that tells the story of our species. Darwin had it right long before anyone knew he did: those who adapt best thrive most. Or, in the simpler and harsher words of Brad Pitt as Billy Beane in the film *Moneyball* to his old-school head scout: "Adapt or die."

These words apply to every aspect of our lives. There is the macro level at which we continue to evolve as a species marching forward through giant swaths of time, and the individual level in which, often without even being aware of it, we show remarkable versatility and malleability during the course of our own personal day-to-day.

Bruce and the Lesson of Ingenuity

Adapt doesn't merely mean "change." Change means "make different"; adapt means "adjust or modify fittingly." To adapt is to change in response to a specific situation, circumstance or need, and an adaptation is any trait or attribute that helps an organism keep on keepin' on, from Alaskan Wood Frogs being able to freeze their bodies solid and stop their hearts during winter to Okapi having infrasonic calls that allow them to communicate with their calves without predators hearing. In Chapter One, we talked about identifying the different parts of your environment, figuring out how to operate most effectively within it, and manipulating its different physical and mental aspects to create the conditions for success. Yes, to achieve your apex, it's critical to put in place as much consistency and predictability as you can. Even more important, however, is to appreciate the need for, and the benefits of, the changes you'll make along the way.

Allow me to tell you the story of a new neighbor, Bruce, whom Nita and I first encountered a short while after we'd moved into our new home in Johns Creek, Georgia. To be fair, I don't know if Bruce was his actual name, since it was the one we gave him after he appeared on a tree branch next to our bird feeder one morning. You see, Bruce was a squirrel. The first time we saw him there, he was for some reason hanging upside-down, like a bat. So we named him Bruce after Bruce Wayne, a.k.a. Batman.

After observing him for a while, we realized this maneuver wasn't just for fun (or to entertain us). Several earlier attempts he had made to get to the food in the squirrel-proof feeder had proven unsuccessful, which made sense, since the thing was indeed designed to be squirrel-proof. In his insistence, however, Bruce had discovered that, by hanging upside-down from a branch just beside the feeder, he could reach the food tray without needing to exert weight on the perch, which would close the access latch. Looking like he was auditioning for Cirque du Soleil, Bruce would pleasantly help himself to snacks knowing he had found the solution to the problem at hand. It doesn't matter if we are watching him, if our dog is barking, or if his sidekick, a chipmunk we named Robin that catches the seeds which fall, is there, Bruce stays focused and intent.

It would be a lie to say we weren't both fascinated by and a little proud of Bruce. We've seen other squirrels climb the same tree, stare at the free buffet, then give up and climb back down. Later, we moved the bird feeder to a different spot Bruce could no longer reach. We also installed a squirrel feeder for him. However, he is still more interested in the bird food, and the chipmunk sidekick has lived up to its name: together they have figured out that the lighter Robin can jump from the same branch, land on the bird feeder without activating the spring, then quickly lay down on the perch and out of harm's way while the pellets get knocked into Bruce's waiting paws below. These two may not exactly be apex animals, however the lesson they continue to reinforce is invaluable: there's more than one way to reach your goals.

The Trade Deadline

Even though the ability to change and respond is so natural an instinct for us, and despite the glorious results it produces, we often resist it in our daily endeavors. We eat the same crappy foods repeatedly even though they make us feel gross and undermine our physical goals. We bump a priority item forever down the to-do list because it isn't fun or interesting or easy, then miss its deadline and get angry with ourselves for having done so. We stick with inefficiencies in our schedule that don't allow us to use our hours as effectively as we could, despite knowing that small modifications could potentially make big differences.

It's an unfortunate truth that, no matter how many times we've achieved success through change, we remain awfully happy to continue doing what we've done – and, without citing the obvious joke about the definition of insanity, let's just agree that, in an embarrassingly high number of situations, we're all guilty of doing the same thing over and over hoping somehow for a different result.

We need to always remind ourselves that evolution doesn't stop, neither for us as a species nor us as individuals. If we stop adapting, we get left behind. Think about it this way. How do you feel about people who dig in during an argument, seeming to have the goal only of wearing the other person down until they admit being wrong? When you are dealing with someone whose help you need to solve a problem, say, getting your car fixed or finding a better cell phone plan, how do you respond when the person goes rigidly by the script and seems unable to step beyond it versus someone more broad in their thinking and committed to finding creative ways to problem-solve?

How do you feel when you realize, after the fact, that you yourself may have been the one who acted stubborn or rigid in a certain situation? Or lazy and complacent? Or myopic and narrow? We know that flexibility, creativity, and the inclination, or at least willingness, to adapt represent the best of us, though we still often catch ourselves demonstrating those other types of traits instead.

Ask yourself these three sets of questions, and answer them honestly:

- ▲ How flexible am I when discussing or debating potential solutions to problems? How much importance do I place on being right, getting my way, or having others agree with me? Do I do this only when I feel I'm right/have the best view, or do I always do it?

- ▲ Are there examples of things I tend to do again and again even though they never yield the results I want? If so, why haven't I changed my approach? Am I intimidated by the effort it would take? Do I hold onto the belief that it will eventually work? Do I just not want to put in the time, even knowing it would be worthwhile?

- ▲ To what extent do I believe I'm fully formed as a human being? How much growing do I believe I still have to do, as opposed to just getting as much done as I can? What are some areas in which I could evolve and broaden myself? Do I actively attempt to evolve and broaden, or do I remain the same me all the time?

The sincere answers to these questions will shed light on how much time you spend, and how much effort you do or don't put into, adapting in pursuit of your goals. You've no doubt heard lots of variations of the axiom that ten percent of life is what happens to us and ninety percent is how we respond or adjust. Don't focus on the things that happen; focus on what you can do about them and the changes that can keep you moving toward the best and most successful version of yourself. Even one of the world's most fearsome predators must keep heading forward to succeed. The great white shark cannot swim backward, only forward, and it must continue swimming in order to keep breathing, since water filtering through its gills provides it with oxygen.

Though we may not have influence over what occurs around us, we have control over how we adjust to those circumstances, in at least three distinct ways:

- ⋏ **Moving on from what isn't working.** Most experts believe that, in our herbivorous ancestors, the appendix was bigger and helped digest the tough stuff we had to eat, such as the bark of trees. While today's plant-eating vertebrates still use the appendix for the same purpose, it's no longer a necessary part of our own digestive system, even though it continues to hang around in there. Remove it and you're fine. (In fact, sometimes it insists on being removed.) There are a number of parts we no longer need, including the tailbone, "wisdom teeth," and the muscle fibers that produce goose bumps. We've moved beyond these evolutionary leftovers, called vestigials, even if it takes significant time for them to disappear from our physiology. (After all, it would be strange if all humans woke up one day to suddenly realize, "Hey, our appendices are gone!") If something is no longer accomplishing what it needs to, move on from it.

- ⋏ **Acquiring or developing new traits.** In the early days of the Internet, a handful of companies developed websites. Not too long after, others did as well, seeing that it could be a good additional tool. It wasn't long before this notion went from "That's kind of interesting, maybe we'll do it, too, if we get around to it" to "Every business obviously needs a website since it's the first place anyone goes." It's easy to fear pushing ourselves into new forms and configurations, yet amazing things can result. Pressurize carbon and you have diamonds. Crush grapes, and you yield wine. Press olives and you get oil. Whenever you feel pressured, crushed, or pressed upon, realize that you're in a powerful place of transformation. All of these things, like you, are unique and valuable in their initial forms, and just as miraculous in their alternate states.

⋀ **Building on what's already there.** Why do people in senior leadership positions keep taking courses and adding degrees? To continue evolving and match the changes in industry, in knowledge, in practices, in people. Why does Microsoft keep releasing new operating platforms and why does Apple keep updating the iPhone? To keep up with evolving customer demands and take advantage of always-improving technology (and to build in obsolescence so that we need to keep buying the new models – discussion for another day). Use the skills and talents you have, and never stop adding to them.

When we're forced to do things differently than we've done, we're given opportunities to build upon ourselves and keep growing. As the famous English writer G.K. Chesterton said, "An inconvenience is only an adventure wrongly considered; an adventure is only an inconvenience rightly considered." The need to adapt opens up chances to find new wells of resourcefulness in ourselves, and to end up in places that surpass our original expectations.

Here's a wonderful example from the 2021 major league baseball season. Leading up to opening day, the Atlanta Braves were predicted to be one of the more successful teams. However, a string of unlikely incidents and injuries started to alter those projections, starting with their best pitcher re-injuring his Achilles tendon during spring training, continuing with one of their top hitters dislocating his fingers in May, and culminating with their emergent superstar tearing his ACL in early July, ending his season and, in the eyes of most, snuffing out any hope the team might have been holding onto as well.

The league's trade deadline of July 31 is circled on the calendar in bright ink by all teams. It is by this date that each must determine whether it is a "buyer" (they will make moves to improve as much as possible for a playoff run) or a "seller" (they will abandon hopes for the season and attempt to build for the future by trading valued assets in exchange for prospects or payroll flexibility). As July 31 arrived, Atlanta had a losing record, though the team had come together and battled its way through four highly challenging months to be sitting only five games out of first place in its division, the New York Mets and Philadelphia Phillies between them and top spot.

The Braves' fans, grateful to the team for its heart and grittiness in "hanging around" this long, bore management no ill will for what would be an expected sell-off at the deadline in hopes of preparing for future success. Instead, Atlanta's brass stunned both the fans and the pundits by becoming an aggressive buyer, adding no fewer than five new players to address the areas where they had been weakened. In one of the most improbable outcomes in recent sports memory, the Braves took over the division lead two weeks later, held onto it until the end of the regular season, won the division series against Milwaukee, defeated the big-market Los Angeles Dodgers to win the National League pennant, then persevered against Houston in the World Series to become league champions for the first time in twenty-six years.

The Braves' lesson is one we all should embrace. When you arrive at inflection points in life, do you become a "buyer" and bet on yourself, believing in your ability to adapt? Treat these moments like Atlanta did its 2021 trade deadline, when management delivered a simple, powerful message: *We believe in the foundation. Let's address the gaps.* You've formulated your goals and made your plans. You've adopted the right mindset, deciding to steam forward with energy and optimism while knowing that bumps in the road will inevitably appear. When they do, it's time to evolve – to discover new sides of you, to plumb new wells of resilience, to force yourself into a new breadth of flexibility, and to create the possibility of amazing outcomes you might not even have imagined.

Lanny's Story

Here in Roswell, Georgia, my wife and I both loved working out, and we belonged to a gym. One day, I was on the website and saw a link that said "Own your Own," with information about becoming a potential franchisee.

We thought it might be an interesting challenge and a cool opportunity. After thinking, talking and researching for several months, we decided to take the plunge.

We opened in October 2016. There's a thriving fitness community here, and we managed to establish a strong clientele fairly quickly. We spent what was necessary to maintain our daily operations and build membership loyalty. Everything else, we saved for a rainy day.

We didn't know that the rainy day would arrive in the form of a global pandemic. When things started to get bad in February 2020, small businesses throughout the country started to close. Then in March, our governor received executive orders to shut down all non-essential services, including gyms. People started sheltering at home and doing their workouts there.

Like other places, we pivoted to delivering services online. Obviously that's complicated for a gym, so it was a quick and unavoidable learning curve, especially since we had basically no online presence. We did everything possible to continue serving our members and keep the community going, from creating a YouTube channel to developing an app from scratch. We posted workouts, delivered new content as frequently as possible, and maintained an ongoing virtual platform to encourage our members to rally together as a community and stay connected.

As a gesture of faith, we also cut membership rates in half, since we recognized that we were offering only half the experience, give or take. A majority of our members stayed, paid the half-rate, and participated as part of this new online community. Some people insisted on continuing to pay the full rate, which touched me.

The nicest expression of community occurred one Saturday morning, when I saw several of our members in the parking lot working out together. They'd decided they just wanted to be at the gym, even if they couldn't be inside. We hadn't organized it; they just made the decision spontaneously. It was such a wonderful statement of resilience and unity. Each Saturday, the crowd grew. They'd come at 6:45 or 7:00 a.m., unprompted. In the midst of the pandemic's constraints, the sight of it was so heartening, and made us feel so grateful. I would go get everything from inside that wasn't bolted down and lend it to members to use at home. Then they'd return it the next weekend for someone else to use for the week.

The forced closure lasted, thank goodness, only two months. In May, we opened again, welcoming our members back into the physical space. We had to modify the way we operated – including social distancing, extra cleaning, and so on. We've maintained those guidelines since, and people have not only adjusted – they tend to prefer it, since the gym would be set up in stations before, and now you kind of have your own equipment in your own space. As far as membership and revenue go, we're back to nearly where we were before Covid.

It was thanks to our willingness to adapt that we were able to ride out this period. It allowed us to survive, and also to foster a shared strength and solidarity in ways we couldn't have foreseen, and which makes our community even stronger today.

Chapter 11: Know What Drives You

Why do we climb mountains? As the old saying goes: because they're there. Though we may not be able to unravel the mystery of why we exist (although *The Hitchhiker's Guide to the Galaxy* says the Answer to the Ultimate Question of Life, the Universe, and Everything, calculated and verified by a specially designed supercomputer over the course of seven and a half million years, is simple: 42), we know we're compelled to explore both our internal selves and the external world. We're motivated to go higher, faster, farther; to get more and more out of ourselves; to see if we can reach the next level, discover the next frontier.

We more often succeed at these pursuits when we know why we're undertaking them. In Chapter Eight, we discussed Alex Honnold, who became the first person to climb the famous wall El Capitan in Yosemite National Park without any gear (it's called "free soloing"). Honnold set this wild goal for himself because, as he put it, he wanted to see if he could achieve total mastery over such an improbable task. Everything he did in preparation was done within the context of that inspiration, including practicing the route countless times, recording in meticulous detail every move to be done throughout the climb of this massive granite wall, and memorizing in precise sequence the specific variety of holds and grips he would need to execute during the nearly four hours it would require to reach the apex.

If It Doesn't Make You Cry, It Isn't A Big Enough Why

You may have heard self-proclaimed gurus refer to the concept of motivation as a lifelong purpose, single all-encompassing reason, or "big why." I disagree with the concept of an overarching why that both applies to all goals and remains the same throughout one's life. Along the route our goals may change, and different inspirations can produce different aspirations. I believe the most important aspects of motivation are the size and impact of what is driving you toward a particular goal at a particular time. I like to think of it as *If it doesn't make you cry, it isn't a big enough why*. In other words, the two vital aspects to your purpose are the specificity of it, and the potential impact on you if you weren't to satisfy it.

Let's talk about the second one first: the effect on you of either hitting a goal or not hitting it. This effect ought to be big. Really big. Your reason for wanting to achieve a goal should not be something you'll be mildly disappointed not to fulfill. It should be something that would feel devastating to fall short of. Honnold made constant sacrifices, big ones, in the single-minded pursuit of climbing El Capitan without ropes. Even the prospect of a fatal slip didn't dampen his motivation. The most upsetting thing about that potential consequence, he said, was that he would feel bad for others having to witness it. Why was that particular individual, at that particular juncture in his life, driven to reach the top of that particular rock wall? Because he couldn't live with the idea of not mastering it.

So, first (or I guess second), your why attached to an individual goal should be big enough that it will crush you not to satisfy it. Second (or I guess first), the why must be specific, because if it isn't defined, you can't use it as your guide. Abstract motivation can be as ineffectual as a vague objective. Establish a concrete and definable purpose to propel you toward the goal you're seeking. See if you can describe it to someone else. An intangible statement like "I want to be seen as a success" doesn't count. A concrete one such as "I want to be debt-free" does.

For hobbies or activities, our reasons don't need to be big, or deep. I once asked a friend why he often gets up early to clear the foliage and debris on his woodland property. He replied, "'Cause I like it." To know you like such an activity is good enough. In fact, "because I like it" is the reason we do a lot of things, especially physical. The endorphin release tells us we like it.

However, in pursuing your apexes, knowing what drives you helps you stay focused on your goals and sustain the effort to meet them. If you're attempting to improve your nutrition and I ask you the reason, "To lose weight" isn't the answer – that's your intended outcome. What's the deeper incentive behind your desire to lose weight? To be able to play with your kids? To live to a certain age? To be attractive to potential partners? To find your abs? If you're deciding to work harder at your job and I ask you why, and you tell me, "To move up in the company," I would ask you to change your answer, because that's an outcome, too. What is truly driving you to do this? To provide for your family? To earn a promotion and increase your salary so that you can pay your mortgage and expenses and start to create savings? To put yourself in a position to do good, since your company makes sustainable environmental products? What's the deep-down impetus for wanting to do what you want to do?

Your motivation for wanting to complete a certain goal isn't necessarily a single one, from a single source. You may draw inspiration from various places, people, events or ideas. By the same token, you may have different incentives which serve as the basis for different goals. There are no rules, no standard-issue one-to-one templates for matching goals to the reasons we want to achieve them. The important thing is that your driving force should be specific enough that you understand it clearly and could explain it to someone else, and it should be big – big enough that you would be crushed to fail.

The Wager, The Daughter and The Marathon (Part 1)

I'd like to share a story with you. In late December 2005, while working in real estate, I was enjoying a vacation in Cabo San Lucas with my colleagues. After working hard all year, we'd surpassed our targets and been rewarded with an all-expenses-paid vacation at this upscale all-inclusive resort, where the days were sunny, the nights were balmy, the food was plentiful, and the alcohol flowed like water. As New Year's Eve approached, we ate, drank, lounged, swam, and enjoyed ourselves to the fullest.

Though on the outside I was putting on a good face, what my colleagues didn't know, what nobody knew, was that I was in a horrible place in my life. I'd gone through a difficult divorce a few years prior, and since, had allowed several dangerous habits to get a foothold and lead me down a slippery slope. I was living on my own and left to my own devices. My daughter was young, and when I'd make her meals and treats, I'd often finish her leftovers after having my own portions. I was going on a series of dates and, for the most part, not enjoying them, since my primary reason for doing so in the first place was to avoid being alone. I wasn't a very big fan of myself then, and so did whatever I could, as often as I could, to avoid my own company. That included going out with friends regularly, and, more often than not, drinking generous amounts. Since I didn't like myself, eating and drinking were the easiest superficial distractions. The worse I ate and the more I drank, the less I thought of myself, and the less

I thought of myself, the more I continued these self-sabotaging behaviors. On and on it went.

By throwing myself into my work, I was making pretty good money – then spending it just as fast on foolish indulgences, spontaneous purchases, and, more than anything else, junk food and alcohol, rather than using it for things like paying off debts or saving for my daughter's future.

I went to therapy for some help digging into my destructive behavior. I believe it was the worst decision I made, because the analyst I met with, despite good intentions, spent most of the time pointing out how the actions of others were responsible for my current tendencies, which directed my negative feelings towards others who didn't deserve it. She was letting me off the hook. What I needed was someone to persuade me to take accountability for myself.

While my teammates and I were dining one evening, one of them mentioned that he had, a few weeks earlier, run the Las Vegas Marathon. Dumbly emboldened by all the alcohol I'd consumed, I heard myself say, "I could do that."

Naturally, all of the others in our group, five of them, teasingly challenged my rash declaration, daring me to do it. The combination of ego and alcohol-driven bravado caused me to repeat the silly claim, and before I knew it, I'd bet each of my five colleagues at the table one hundred dollars that I could complete the following year's marathon. I'm about five-foot-ten. At the time, I weighed two hundred and forty-five pounds. (At the time of this writing, I'm a hundred sixty-one.) Not quite peak shape for running 26.2 miles.

When we arrived home a few days later, I got a phone call from our preferred lender, who asked if I was still taking wagers. It seemed my stupid bet had made its way through the grapevine. I accepted his bet, too. That made six bets of one hundred dollars each. The most I'd ever run at one time was playing football with my friends.

My first step was the one you'd expect: buying some cool running gear. Now I was outfitted to succeed – perfect. Of course, those clothes sat in a drawer for all of January. When February showed up, I'd neither unwrapped the purchases nor even walked a mile. So I took the next reasonable step: bought an expensive treadmill, using the partial justification that I usually had my daughter to care for, so running at home would be easiest. That proved highly useful – as a clothing rack for the running gear I'd finally taken out of its packaging. February passed. Still I'd done not a minute of training.

In March, I decided it was time to get serious. (Of course, doing anything would have meant being more serious than I'd been so far.) My daughter was with me that day. I put her in front of the TV, then put on my running clothes and got on the treadmill, draping a towel over the display so I didn't have to see how slowly the time would go. I started running. Sped up a little, then a little more. After a while, dripping sweat and gasping for air, I hit the emergency stop and, as I was catching my breath, triumphantly yanked the towel off, impressed with myself. I'd gone only half a mile.

I collapsed onto the treadmill and started to cry.

Simone came into the room, saw me weeping, and walked up to me. She put her hand on my shoulder, looked at me with her big brown eyes, and said, "Daddy, you can do anything you put your mind to."

She was echoing back to me what I'd been telling her since she was born. Before that moment, I'd had no why, no purpose to bring me back up and drive me forward. In the instant my little daughter said those words, my why became clear. I had to either do what I'd been teaching her or admit I was a liar. If it doesn't make you cry, it isn't a big enough why.

I spent every day between that one and the date of the marathon dedicated to living my truth to Simone. Validating her belief in me was a more profound motivation for me than the bets, the money, or my own pride, and letting her down would have broken my heart. Every time thereafter that I stepped on the treadmill, every change I made to my diet, every daunting step toward toeing that starting line, was about her. When she was with me, I'd run on the treadmill. When she wasn't, I'd run outside. No matter what, I ran. I joined a running club to help me train better and draw from the support of others.

By mid-October, I'd lost sixty-five pounds. Two weeks before the marathon, one of my teammates, on behalf of the rest of the group, approached me smiling, and held out an envelope. I opened it to see five crisp hundred-dollar bills. "I don't understand," I said. "I haven't run the marathon."

"Doesn't matter," she said. "As far as we're concerned, you've already succeeded."

Find your why. Reach for the sky.

Lucas's Story

I was born in Lawrence, a town in northeast Kansas, and later moved to Houston to take a prominent role within a Ministry. I discovered early, as early as age sixteen, that I had a natural talent for preaching, in particular to groups. I hosted a TV show as a senior, moved on to preaching within my Ministry for a few years, and eventually led a church of my own, where I was able to speak to larger and larger crowds.

I got married, had four wonderful kids, kept ascending up through the Ministry. One day, I was on stage in Indiana preaching to a crowd of fifty thousand. That evening, I had a video call with my kids, said goodnight, told them I loved them, turned off the computer, and decided something had to change. I was seeing them more often on video than in person. It wasn't right. I could no longer bear the distance from them.

A short time later, I was flipping channels on TV, and came upon the show House Hunters. I thought to myself, "This might be something I could do" (though I now understand there's nothing "real" about that or any "reality" show). I was desperate. As I said, I'd started preaching at sixteen, and it was the only thing I knew, the only world I'd ever been a part of. My degree was a Bachelor of Science in Pastoral Ministries. I was virtually unemployable. I got my real estate license, hoping for the best, willing to do whatever it took to continue providing for my family while also being physically present with them.

Gaining a foothold in Houston in real estate in 2008 was, to put it mildly, a nightmare. It's an oil and energy town, and gas was in a terrible place. Energy companies were laying people off left, right and center. Foreclosures were happening everywhere. It was the worst place at the worst time. In addition, the learning curve was steep. I had to learn both the business side and the marketing side of real estate in parallel. I promised myself I wouldn't market to anyone from my Ministry world, so one of the biggest changes was separating Reverend Lucas from Realtor Lucas. I was starting completely cold. Regardless, I was in it. We had four kids ranging between sixth grade and junior high and I pledged to myself that I wasn't going to let them down.

It didn't start well. A year or so in, I had done only one transaction and was $100,000 in debt. When people asked me if I was interested in their guidance, I tended to avoid or decline it. I was stubborn; I wanted to succeed on my own. People would ask me things like, "How's the market?" and I would say something self-deprecating such as "How would I know?"

On one of these occasions, my daughter overheard me, and said, "You're a good realtor, aren't you, Daddy?" I heard myself reply to her aloud, "Yes, Honey, I am," and then I heard, in my head, *But I wasn't ten seconds ago.* From that moment on, my only goal was to make the statement I'd made to her true.

I committed to doing everything within my power to live up to this declaration I'd given her. Door-knocking. Cold-calling. Anything. Everything. I would stop pushing back against those who offered help or advice.

Listening to others helped enormously. I came to understand that in real estate, there's no such thing as a good or bad market. There is only the market that exists at the time, because that's the one you need to work with, adapt to, and find opportunity in. One of my fellow realtors shared with me the famous story of the two shoe salesmen sent to Africa to assess the market. One reports, "No one wears shoes here. There's no market." The other says, "No one wears shoes here. There's nothing but opportunity!"

I also embraced the fact that there are daily acts one must do to plant the seeds for success. Mastery of the process and achievement of success largely involve the will to do these activities consistently, even when they feel mundane. Do you get awards for managing your balance sheet every week or doing a certain number of hours of lead-generation? No. To use a baseball analogy, those are the singles and doubles that, collectively, lead to runs, and victories.

At the start of each day, I would remind myself of the question my daughter had asked, and the answer I'd given. Then I reminded myself that success was attainable based on my attitude toward it, my willingness to be humble, and my ability to stay focused on my ultimate, non-negotiable purpose: taking care of the people who mattered most to me in the world.

Over the next nine months, I made thirty-two transactions. I ultimately ended up running, then buying, one of our firm's offices. It was all because I made an unequivocal decision: that greatness doesn't occur when I feel like it. It isn't defined by waking up to find a bunch of deals falling in my lap. It's defined by placing one stone after another in the river and making steady, continued progress. I learned how to identify promising opportunities for clients. I learned how to work effectively within the market and anticipate fluctuations. I learned about the value of rental properties and accumulated enough capital to buy one of my own, and eventually sell it for a significant profit.

Today, I own offices in multiple states, and people come to me with listings, rather than the other way around. I am taking care of my family, and I am around for my kids. People ask me what were the most important changes or decisions I made to get from there to here. There are three. The first was that simple yet momentous change in mindset – going from focusing on the forces seeming to act upon me from outside to focusing instead on the steps I can take to drive my own success. You can't sit around feeling bad and hoping to get a stroke of good fortune. You need to create it yourself. The second thing was getting rid of that stubbornness that made me want to do it on my own and resist others' wisdom. Getting humble goes a long way. I now not only welcome advice from others, I invite it. Finally, I always kept in the forefront of my mind that statement I'd made to my daughter. What drove me every single day was keeping that promise to her.

Chapter 12: Stretch Your Goals

"Stretch goals" are complicated. Failing forward, progress through obstacles, partial success – while these terms all make sense, there's a subtle balance between faltering just enough to keep inspiring us and setting unreasonable expectations that set us up for disappointment. The first scenario means you set goals that, though distant and challenging, you can envision yourself meeting. The second means you define vague and random objectives that only serve to demoralize you.

A critical aspect of this is understanding – and acknowledging – what is within your control and what is not. I dislike when people are encouraged to create "goal" lists that include such statements as "I'll be a millionaire in five years." That's certainly a nice thing to aim for, except your ambition isn't the only factor influencing it, so it's unfair. An example of a fair statement is "I will put half of every paycheck into savings." That's an act no one controls except you. Every goal you set, easy, medium or hard, should be squarely within your scope of influence.

The Three Levels of Goal-Setting

I encourage people to divide their goals into three levels: Comfortable, Possible and Improbable. Comfortable goals are those you're confident you can meet, and that you're also likely to meet without any special effort or challenge. Such goals are important in our lives. Those things you often hear described as "quick wins" or "low-hanging fruit" have value, because they produce small ongoing rewards and continuing bits of positive reinforcement along the path to the bigger goals we wish to tackle.

Comfortable isn't the level at which the majority of your goals should be set, yet it's where most people set them. Why? Because unconsciously it's more satisfying to set goals we know we'll hit, then high-five ourselves when we do. It takes the possibility of failure or disappointment out of the conversation, which is nice. The issue is, of course, that it also removes the possibility of growth, improvement and the unique high of pushing beyond what's easy or comfortable, and experiencing the rewards that come with doing so. There has been extensive research in recent years on the science and art of motivation. One of the things this research shows is that the setting of easily achievable goals can significantly limit motivation, and that it shows in the results, or lack of them. If you know you're going to hit your annual target by Halloween, there's little point in exerting much effort for the rest of the year, since it doesn't benefit you any further.

That's where we come to Possible goals. Think of these as what are often called "reach" goals – those that are harder than Comfortable, those which you're only partially confident you can meet, those that make you equally nervous and excited to aim for because you're equally certain and uncertain of your ability to attain them.

Possible goals are the last few reps you squeeze out of a set when you're exercising. When I'm following a program, I prefer the instructor to tell me to do a given set of a specific move to failure rather than going for a specific number of reps – because if I can manage that number of reps, I'm happy with my temporary achievement, yet all I've met is a Comfortable goal. It's when you power through those last two or three pushups, or those last few seconds of a plank, or those last few I'm-seriously-going-to-die burpees, that true growth is triggered. When I'm told that twelve is my limit, that's the ceiling I'm aiming for. Being forced to define my ceiling as I go makes me mentally and physically strive toward new thresholds all the time. One of my baseball coaches used to teach us that, instead of making first base your goal when you're running up the line, aim for five feet past it. That way, you'll run through the base at full speed rather than slowing down as you cross it because you viewed it as your destination. Possible goals are the same. They help you continue to move the yardsticks.

Improbable goals are big stretches – those in which the stars need to align in just the right way, in combination with your own effort and drive, to be realized. It's just as important to have Improbable goals as it is to have Comfortable ones. Comfortable goals are there to keep showing us what we can accomplish day to day, and to create ongoing momentum, energy and confidence; Possible goals, to make us reach beyond what we're used to and constantly push our limits; Improbable goals, to inspire the big visions and leaps of faith that create the possibility of achieving dreams.

Possible goals are the sweet spot where you should focus most of your energy and effort. Comfortable goals require little of you, and will likely be met; Improbable goals require a lot of you, and still entail tall odds.

Possible goals force you to constantly redefine your boundaries. Even if you fall short, in making it your aim, you're still exceeding what would otherwise be a Comfortable level. If the proverbial carrot is placed too close to the donkey, he will hardly need to move to get it; if it's placed a little further, he will keep pulling the cart all day long; if it's placed too far, he may give up or not attempt to get it at all.

This is the pattern that leads to growth and enrichment: setting Possible goals, striving for them through planning, effort and sustained commitment, then, once you've reached them and brought them to Comfortable level, defining new goals to force you toward new heights. If the majority of your objectives are in the Comfortable zone, you're enabling your own complacency. Make it normal to set goals that aren't easy to meet, or that you may not meet the first time, so that you can appreciate when you do hit them. If I bend over to touch my toes, I may not be able to do it the first time. Yet I persist. I relax, stand back up, and do it again. With each attempt, my hamstrings loosen a little more, and I bring the goal closer within my reach (literally). Eventually, I succeed, and it's time to define the next challenge.

Today, a marathon might feel like a long run. Heck, a 5K might feel like a long run. So run to the end of your street and back today. Tomorrow, run around your block one time. Next week, run through the neighborhood for fifteen minutes. Before you know it, the 5K that seemed like an improbability for you has become comfortable – at which point it's time to set a new goal.

Speaking of marathons, in case you're wondering how things turned out…

The Wager, The Daughter and The Marathon (Part 2)

In Chapter Eleven, I shared the story about my foolishly declaring out of alcohol-induced audacity that I could run a marathon, then having to actually train to do so to make good on the doubly foolish wager I'd made about it with my colleagues. They had paid up before the marathon even arrived, saying the commitment I'd made to improving myself was success enough in their eyes.

For me, though, only completing the race would mean validating the words of my daughter, who had told me I can do anything I put my mind to. I was happy to have improved my physical state, pleased to have corrected the bad habits that had sunk me into a vicious cycle, and filled with a feeling of vigor and lightness I hadn't known in years. However, the Las Vegas Marathon now loomed, and if I didn't do what I said I'd do, it wasn't the ill-informed alcohol-induced declaration to my teammates I'd be failing, it was my why: Simone's faith that I could do it.

Actually, not everyone had paid me. Scott, our preferred lender, the one who had joined the wager after I'd returned home from Cabo San Lucas, called again to offer me double or nothing. "I know you're going to do it," he said. "I want to know how fast. Let's bet on that."

Without much thought, I heard myself say, "Four hours, thirty minutes."

"You're on," he said, pretty happy about the time I'd declared, which was just about as impulsive as saying I could run the thing in the first place.

On the day of the race, there I stood, at one end of the famed Vegas Strip, feeling ready, or at least as ready as any first-timer can feel. The group I'd trained with was there alongside me, helping with both moral support and practical guidance. The race announcer counted us down. Because of the thousands of participants, it took me more than seven minutes to reach the actual starting line. Once there, I started my stopwatch and, competitive juices flowing, sped up a little almost immediately, in response to which my teammates advised me just as quickly to pace myself and avoid burning out early. I slowed down – apparently too much, as they then told me I should speed up. Finally I found what felt like the sweet spot.

Around Mile 3, some of those in our group starting falling off the pace. By Mile 6, where the race splits off from The Strip, I realized I'd lost the whole group. Miles 7 and 8 are an uphill climb, which not only did I not mind, I embraced, since I loved running hills and had been trained to attack them. I passed everyone on that section, loving the high, feeling fantastic. Then I watched all those same people pass me over the next section because of the energy I'd expended on the hill climb.

Mile 13 is important in a marathon, because it's the halfway point. At the precise halfway mark, 13.1 miles, there's a big clock that tells you your time. I was at over two hours, which meant the winner of the race had already finished.

Around mile 16, I wasn't sure I could keep running. I started bartering with myself. *I'll run to that Stop sign. I'll walk to that street light. No, the next street light.* I'd run one section and then walk the next, run, walk, run, walk. At Mile 20, I felt no excitement at the 2 in front of the number, since there were still six miles left to run, which felt like sixty.

Mile 23 was memorable because the water station was for some reason also dispensing beer. I saw three runners standing there drinking beer and the coach in me encouraged them to press on. "Come on, guys, we're almost there!" I shouted. "Let's get this!" They joined me – though after about four steps, one of them went down, having pulled something. A second fell apart a short time later, withdrawing from the race, and the third guy soon said he wanted to go back for the other two. I was alone again.

Nearing the last mile marker, I approached the corner at a not-quite-brisk walk. Walk, run, walk, run, all the way to the finish. It isn't the first 26 miles that kills you; it's the last 0.2. The course was set up so that, at Mandalay Bay, we made a turn for the final two-tenths of a mile and ran across the hotel parking lot, which was fenced in. Even though it was a marathon, this was Las Vegas, so the finish line was a big, glitzy party.

I'd asked my ex-wife if she would bring my daughter to the finish line, since she was the reason I had started this journey in the first place – she was my why. I looked around, not seeing her. My vision the entire time had been to pick her up and carry her across the finish line. Finally, straight ahead, I saw her on the other side of it, holding up a sign that read, in multiple colors and covered with glitter, DADDY, YOUR THE BEST. The cute mistake made it even more beautiful.

I put my head down and sprinted the remainder. Passing the finish line, I grabbed Simone, lifted her to the air, and twirled her around. When one of the race organizers approached me with my completion medal, he asked Simone, "Would you like to put this on him?" She did, then they took our photo together. That photo shows both the most exhausted and most exhilarated smile of my life.

I was also so elated in that moment, and so focused on finding my daughter in the crowd, that I'd forgotten to stop my watch, so I didn't know my finishing time. I remembered that all participants get a tracker placed on their bib at the beginning of the race to prevent cheating, and all times are posted on the race website, so after driving home and downing a pizza (yes, a whole pizza, and yes, by myself), I immediately went to the website and entered my ID number. While my start time and halfway time were there, the finish time hadn't yet been uploaded. I sat at the computer refreshing the screen every thirty seconds for a while, never seeing it update. (The Internet has come a long way since then.) Finally, I gave up and collapsed into bed, sank into a beautiful deep sleep, and woke up in the morning feeling happy, albeit fairly stiff.

Once I got out of bed, I realized "fairly stiff" was actually more like "barely able to move." It took me so long to get out of the house that I forgot to check the website. When I finally arrived at the office, I saw a plain white envelope on my desk with the words "You suck" written on the front. Opening it, I found two crisp hundred-dollar bills and a slip of paper that read, *Chad Hyams, 4:29:39.*

After wiping away my tears – very different tears than the ones I'd shed after my first attempt on the treadmill eight months earlier – I immediately did two things. First, I called my daughter to thank her for helping me find my purpose. Second, I signed up for another marathon.

Justin's Story

When I was young, my dad was in the Navy, so we moved around quite a bit – from Charlotte, South Carolina, to Newport News, Virginia, then to Huntsville, Alabama, then, when I was fourteen, to Mobile. I have an older sister and two younger brothers, all of whom were naturally smart and academically successful and well behaved at home. I felt like the black sheep. I believed I was smart, even if not book smart.

In my teens, I entered a pretty rebellious period, copping an attitude toward authority, messing around at school, defying my parents...I was feeling pretty dark in general. I don't know exactly why. Maybe a combination of all that moving around combined with watching my siblings get good grades, behave well, go to college, and do everything else that was expected, while at the same time I wasn't sure who I was or where I was headed.

When I was about eighteen, there was a moment that changed me. Even though it was something mundane, it affected me powerfully. I was having a bad day, driving to school, kind of unaware of anything apart from my own toxic mood, when I realized there was a lady in a nearby parking lot who was blocked from getting out onto the main road due to a line of traffic at the stoplight. I looked over and saw how frustrated she seemed. As the line began to move, I decided to let her in. She nodded and waved thanks. Just like that, it was as though I rediscovered a sense of empathy. I felt my insides shift to the positive.

In my late teens, I got into acting, doing some minor background and stand-in work in a few small films. At twenty-one, I moved to Atlanta for a small role in a slightly bigger-budget film, and found myself with much more down time than I was expecting. At the time, I was staying with my uncle, who had an acquaintance who had been on the show American Ninja Warrior and owned a Ninja Warrior training facility. I asked him what I'd need to do to come in and give it a go. He let me come in one day, and I was immediately hooked. I begged him for a job. Eventually, he let me start to train as a coach.

I'd always been naturally slight. I wasn't very strong, wasn't overly athletic, and had a hard time putting on muscle. My background was in coaching gymnastics. At this time, ninja training wasn't yet popular. People only knew ninjas from movies and the TV show, which was gaining in popularity. When I started training, most of those around me were extremely strong – predominantly weightlifters and CrossFitters with tremendous upper body strength, something I lacked severely. Something told me to go for it anyway. I decided to start training anyway, with the goal of making it onto the show. I knew it was beyond what was comfortable or familiar for me, but I wanted to give it my best shot.

It was disheartening at first. People would tell me, for example, just hold yourself up with one arm. I couldn't. I wanted to be a coach in this industry, though I couldn't walk the talk. I felt like I had this inherent lack of strength that would always keep me at a disadvantage. Despite not being particularly strong myself, I proved to be a competent coach, and, over time, worked my way up to the position of director of the gym's Ninja training program.

However, other aspects of my life were coming apart. I'd started dating a girl who had kids, and had moved in with her. I found out later that she wasn't paying her rent. She, or I guess we, got evicted, followed by an ugly breakup. After sleeping in my car for a few nights, I went to the gym to stay. The same evening, I got a call from my grandma, who told me to come stay with her and my grandpa. They lived an hour south, in

McDonough, Georgia. I accepted, feeling like a failure. I ended up staying with them for two months.

Two significant things happened during that time, both thanks to my grandfather. First, he introduced me to martial arts. I'd done parkour and gymnastics when I was younger because, as the skinny kid who wouldn't be able to fight anyone, I figured I'd instead make it hard for people to catch me. Martial arts was a natural extension of parkour, and I connected with it right away.

The second thing grandpa did was give me a book called *The 4-Hour Work Week*, which is about finding a different way than the typical 9-to-5, work-at-a-desk, put-in-endless-hours, save-for-retirement path. That spoke to me, too. It helped give me confidence that I could succeed using a less conventional path.

I started thinking, Okay, what comes easily to me? What am I good at? I remembered this move I'd come upon while doing gymnastics training called the Glide Kip. As a gymnastics coach, I'd seen young girls doing it, and had felt so frustrated being unable to do it myself that I dedicated myself to mastering the skill. I started practicing it over and over until I could get it, and, while practicing, thought about the principles of perfecting the move. It wasn't just about strength; it was equally about rhythm and momentum, moving your body through space in an efficient way. It was a revelation for me. Soon I started being able to perform moves and get through obstacles that most others who were much more muscular and "stronger" than me couldn't. And the ones who could often looked clunky or forced. I looked smooth and efficient.

After about two years, I moved back to the Mobile area to study business and resume gymnastics coaching. Not long after, I was contacted by an old friend in Huntsville who had recently opened a Ninja Academy. He offered me a position that would allow me to run the academy and become a part-owner in the company. I accepted and moved back to Huntsville. After taking a while to get a foothold, people started to discover us, and the business started to flourish.

Having reconnected with my gymnastics roots, I applied the concept of capitalizing on momentum, biomechanics and physics to start developing a training program of my own, using six foundational moves. The program's philosophy is about mastering technique for repeated success, as opposed to focusing on short-term results. It's a more intellectual approach to athleticism, based on training the neurons and building muscle memory. The more disciplined you become, the more freedom you have.

What was initially perceived as a disadvantage (the inability to hurl myself through the air using upper body strength alone) would ironically become the foundation for the training system we now use. Once I changed my perspective and embraced a more innovative approach, things turned around. It's precisely because I wasn't able to "just do it" that I was able to figure out exactly what was necessary to get "it" done successfully every time. And since we know what needs to be done step by step, we can accurately teach those steps to anyone. Five years after assuming the role, I can proudly say that thousands of people have come through my academy and learned how to move more freely, more comfortably, and more confidently. The lesson I learned is that sometimes weakness is merely a matter of perspective – and that you don't need to be like everyone else to find your own path. Aim as high as you can, and stretch your vision as far as it will go.

Chapter 13: Ask the Right Questions

In previous chapters, we've talked about pushing yourself to aim for big goals, preparing for the inevitable pivots and adjustments along the way, and doing it all with a firm purpose. Of all the different ways we maintain this pursuit of our apex – the physical, the practical, the strategic, the tactical – the most important is the mental. And of the different mental exercises we do to keep ourselves moving toward that peak – the mantras we repeat, the meditation we practice, the visualizations we undertake – the most important of these is the ongoing act of self-motivation. One of the greatest motivational speakers, Zig Ziglar, puts it like this: "People often say that motivation doesn't last. Well, neither does bathing, that's why we recommend it daily."

It's simple enough to work backward from a goal and determine a logical plan for meeting it. It's a welcome challenge to design the details of such a plan, laying out steps, timelines and milestones. And if the plan is designed well, executing it becomes a fairly straightforward effort, too.

The psychological game we play against ourselves, however, is never so simple. Our big brains allow us advanced cognition, sophisticated ideas, and awesome acts of innovation and invention. Those brains also produce a level of complexity that has a way of messing with us, since they produce both confidence and doubt, excitement and alarm, composure and unease, eagerness and apprehension. The number-one fear among humans is public speaking, for goodness' sake. How strange is that for a species whose members survive on communicating with one another? Yep – we're not easy on ourselves.

We look to many sources to help us win the ongoing motivational battle. Songs. Sayings. Posters. Pep talks. One of the most popular techniques for pushing through uncertainty or anxiety is self-affirmations. You know them – those optimistic statements or phrases meant to transform the negative or unhelpful thoughts that creep in and take root. *I'm great at my job. I make healthy choices. My relationships are solid. I am in control of my life.*

We're told to repeat these carefully crafted self-testimonials often, so that, eventually, we come to believe them, and behave accordingly. They are composed in present tense. They are always positive. And they are intended to be as personal and specific as possible (even if the catchphrase of the most popular and funniest proponent of them, Stuart Smalley from Saturday Night Live fame, was entertainingly general: "I'm good enough, I'm smart enough, and doggone it, people like me!").

These declarations of personal worth and ability started to become fashionable in the late 1980s, the theory being that, if repeated enough, they could help break down thoughts or notions that threatened one's concept of self. Some studies implied that self-affirmations could help people cope with things like academic pressure, health problems, and defensiveness. It was suggested that, because we're always driven to protect our concept of self-integrity, since we want to believe we're good, moral people who act in ways aligned to cultural and social norms, and given our need to feel like intelligent, altruistic, self-sufficient members of a productive and kind society, any experiences or messages that contradict these instincts do damage, and we need to counter them with reminders of our own value and ability.

My belief about self-affirmations is that, in most cases, they are counter-productive, and furthermore, that, rather than being magically self-fulfilling prophecies that enable self-actualization, they're hollow statements and convenient lies which encourage complacency. They provide false comfort because they're dull, empty and obvious. For every one of these bland affirmations we speak, our brains give the same response: *Sure, if you say so.*

This kind of uninterested reply is not the kind we want from our own minds when we're attempting to light an internal fire. Generic pronouncements about our own worth or potential encourage us to avoid accountability. And if you ask me (which you sort of did since you're still reading), there is nothing any of us ought to demand of ourselves more than accountability, in every part of life, every day. Don't just tell yourself you're doing great. Challenge yourself to see how great you can be.

So how do you turn these flimsy self-affirmations into words of substance and meaning? Through a simple trick: converting them into questions, called *askfirmations*, which help make the nebulous concrete and turn the passive active. A typical, standard self-affirmation carries no consequence, whereas a question demands an answer. Questions are potent; they lead to change. Why? Because when we really get our brains involved in a task, when we truly engage, we are triggered not merely to think. We are also forced to act.

When you're attempting to place a certain actor whose name you can't quite remember, you don't say to yourself, "I know the name of this actor." You ask yourself who it is. You think about other films this actor has been in as a way of loosening the possibilities. You experiment with different letter sounds and fragments to help stimulate the neural pathways. Often, the name comes to you hours later – the end result of that initial activity you spurred simply by asking your brain to pursue the answer.

Telling yourself "I'm healthy" doesn't make you healthy. Saying "I'm a success" doesn't make you one. Declaring "I will exercise today" isn't likely to cause you to do it. Repeating "I will make a million dollars" over and over doesn't make it come true. Reframing these statements into questions challenges you to come up with, and act on, the answers:

"What can I do to be healthier? What time will I exercise today? What kind of exercise will I do? For how long?"

"What defines success for me, and what are the steps I need to take to achieve it? What can I do today to move closer to achieving my goal?"

"What will it require of me to make a million dollars? What is a reasonable time frame for achieving this goal? How do I go about it?"

Making false, blanket assertions absolves you from any responsibility in making them true, whereas asking questions like those above is like removing the rock that starts an avalanche, except what you're activating is a cascade of mental action that then starts a chain reaction of actual behaviors. The statements are meaningless and empty; the questions contain unlimited power and potential.

As you continue to ask yourself these questions, the answers can take various forms. And as these answers build, so do the behaviors that make them a reality. You might ask yourself the same question every few months in pursuit of a particular goal. A self-affirmation such as "I'm wealthy" is static and irrational. The question, "What can I do today to get me closer to this financial goal?" is both tangible and dynamic. It doesn't only demand an initial response, it also kicks off of a continuing process of momentum. While affirmations exist in a vacuum, askfirmations spark answers that evolve as you move forward. By asking yourself how you will perform better at your job, or grow in your relationships, or eventually do a perfect handstand, you are also asking what will be different when you ask yourself the same question again in a week, a month, or a year.

The questions should be direct, and they should be difficult. Don't let yourself off the hook with easy ones. Give them weight. Make them count. As a friend of mine wrote recently, "At some point you gotta be real with yourself about the gap between the life you want to live and the life that your daily habits are leading you towards." Research shows that asking questions both helps focus our thinking and creates flexibility in the exploration of answers. Pre-formed statements close that possibility off. Questions throw it wide open.

To make the changes you want to make, to take real, meaningful strides toward your apex, you need to confront who you are today, right now, and think about who you want to be tomorrow and in the future. Do it in an honest and uncompromising way. Asking clear questions, and demanding plain answers, helps refine your habits, guide your decisions, and focus your behaviors. Questions aren't just powerful; they're empowering. Ask them of yourself, and insist upon the answers.

Shay's Story

I used to be really big on affirmations. I would read the books, listen to the videos, repeat the mantras to myself: you're a great mom, you're a great wife, you're great at your job, you're a millionaire. Then I connected with a coach, who asked me, Are you really all those things? Just by saying it, are you becoming it? Do you really believe you're a great mom, a great wife, great at your job? How is it that you're telling yourself you're a millionaire if you're not? He was pretty no-nonsense in his view that I was telling myself pointless lies. He suggested I take these same statements and see if it might help to put them in question form. He knew that by doing so I could frame them as concrete goals to work toward, as opposed to empty statements that – he was right – were false.

I broke it down – the changes made were simple, and powerful. For example, instead of saying "I'm a millionaire," which, let's face it, I definitely wasn't, I said, "What can I do today to become a millionaire?"

Instead of just telling myself I'm a great wife and mother, I looked in the mirror and decided I was actually doing pretty poorly at both those roles. So I changed them both to questions: "What can I do to become a better wife and mother?" And similarly, "What can I do to become more successful at my job?"

I placed these questions on my computer home screen in rotation, so that I'd see them every day and be forced to answer. Every day, I ask them to myself, out loud, and almost every day, I come up with different answers. For example, in really confronting the question about what kind of wife I am, I came to realize I wasn't a very good listener with my husband. I didn't like when he was right about things and would often avoid conversations, or just tune out. I don't need to tell you that's pretty counterproductive to a good spousal relationship. I made myself acknowledge that he was putting in more than I was. I also didn't have a very affectionate relationship with my mom growing up, and I wanted to change that history with my own daughter. Finally, I didn't feel I was truly fulfilling my potential at work. I thought I could experience success by believing I could just speak it into existence – as opposed to acting it into existence.

While the shift in mentality was, as I said, seemingly small, seemingly simple, the results have been profound, professionally and personally. My husband has complimented me on how much I've changed, and frequently tells me how much he appreciates the little things I'm doing to be more present and connected. I'm tuned in to my daughter's love language, and I understand that spending time with her is the biggest gift I can give as a parent. I now make sure to carve out part of every day to make that happen. We walk the dog, we play a game, we sing a song. We dance together every day. I've become more proactive at work, talking to clients, asking for their feedback, making more calls, paying attention to what the most successful people around me do every day.

My routine now is get up, do yoga, engage in some positive visualizations, then go through those askfimations. Like I said, I come up with different answers every day. The point is asking the questions!

Chapter 14: Build Good Habits

Allow me to start this chapter by stating something obvious.

Good habits lead to positive results.

Obvious, right? Reading those words, you likely scoffed a little, rolled your eyes, or maybe said something like, *Thanks for the news, Chad. Did you think of that one on your own?*

Of course I didn't. Everyone knows it's true, and we hear, see and read variations of it all the time. Such principles are so straightforward, in fact, that they should also be simple to implement. What makes them so hard? We're human, and we live in a modern world full of conveniences, luxuries, distractions and temptations. Building good habits takes work. Consistent work. Lots of it. On the surface, it's easy. Being in shape requires a healthy diet and regular exercise? You bet, no problem. Succeeding in business demands ongoing focus and calculated risks? I can do that. Sustaining a relationship takes active communication and emotional availability? Sounds like a plan.

It's easy to say these things. Intuitively, we get it. The formulas seem so simple, how could we not? Yet often we find that the traits for building these good habits – commitment, focus, tenacity – are difficult to put into practice. Let's look a little closer at why this is, and what you can do to establish consistent habits that will help you achieve your apex.

A House of Habits

We're often told to look at the big picture. In philosophical terms, I agree. When it comes to practical measures and behaviors, however, it's more useful to break the picture down and tackle it in pieces. When you think about all the different things you want to accomplish, your big goals, your life aims, they can be overwhelming. Approaching those goals step by step, day by day, makes them more manageable, and, more important, allows you to appreciate your progress in a more tangible way. When you set for yourself one huge goal, it can feel like an ever-receding horizon you can't quite reach and that never really comes into focus. In contrast, when you concentrate on the process and the daily habits you're embedding, you enter a cycle of ongoing motivation and results that bring the goal closer and closer.

When I ask you how you use your hours, a lot of things probably come to mind. If I ask you whether you use them well, the answer may feel even more complex. Using time well isn't so easy to define, even though we kind of know when we're doing it, or not doing it.

There are two components to using your hours well: productivity and efficiency. Applying both equals what I call constructive time. When you use your hours both productively and efficiently, you're building progress toward a goal. Each habit or behavior is like a different piece of that progress, the way each part of building a house contributes to the final result. One habit represents the frame; another, wiring and insulation; a third, plumbing; a fourth, the roof, and so on. The whole is you; the individual parts are your habits and behaviors, each contributing to the overall result. Start to embed them a little at a time, one day after another, and before too long, you've built a house. No matter how big or small the house you want to build, no matter how simple or fancy, the process is the same.

The construction of a house is a big enterprise, just like pursuing big goals in our lives. Doing so often feels daunting because, well, there simply doesn't seem to be enough time to do everything such ambitions require.

Usually, we can find more time when we put our average day under a microscope and have a closer look. Most of us have more "waste" time in our schedule than we think. When you identify and adjust even a few of these, you might be surprised at how many minutes, even hours, you find yourself retrieving. Ever watch an hour-long TV show during its regular broadcast? That requires sixty minutes of your time. Ever record it so you can watch it later? That might instead take fifty minutes, since you can fast-forward through the commercials. Ever wait to watch that same show on a streaming service or a few days later when it's available on demand without commercials altogether? That sixty-minute show is now just forty-two minutes long. You've gained eighteen minutes. It may not seem like much in isolation. Do that same exercise a few times, however, and it adds up.

Combining activities can also help – tying one habit to another to increase productivity and efficiency at the same time. What if you were to do a few sets of squats every time you brush your teeth? What about keeping a bottle of water in the car and taking three healthy swigs each time you get in? (Or get out, so you don't drink too much while driving and then need to find a restroom.) One activity triggers the other. Think about your typical day and ask yourself in what ways you could tie one activity to another to embed a new habit that moves you closer to your apex.

Soap Operas, Cheat Meals and The Power of Doing Nothing

Productivity involves getting things done; efficiency, using your time in effective ways. Are you filling your hours with fruitful activities that yield positive effects, or do you find yourself spending most of the time doing things like watching soap operas, eating unhealthy meals at restaurants, or, as my dad was fond of saying, sitting around watching the grass grow?

Now, hang on. There can be value to watching trashy TV, enjoying a cheat meal, or partaking in active forms of what is sometimes referred to as "nothing," like watching the grass grow. Such activities can represent healthy periods of mental and psychological relaxation, centering and detachment. The important difference is whether you make the choice to do "nothing" for a specific period of time or realize after a period of time that you've done nothing. The first scenario is often accompanied by feelings of renewal and invigoration; the second, by feelings of guilt and self-doubt.

How do your daily habits and activities serve your personal big picture? Watching that soap may be something you've earmarked as an activity of value because it's your preferred guilty pleasure after working hard all day. You've made that choice in an active way – as opposed to, again, sitting up off the couch after two hours of watching soap operas and realizing you weren't even really conscious of doing it. Those kinds of behaviors can lead down hazardous roads because they can spark a vicious cycle whereby an unproductive behavior is followed by feelings of shame at having engaged in that behavior, followed by similar behaviors engaged in as self-punishment, and so on. Whereas if you decide, "I'm going to watch trainwreck TV for an hour before making dinner as a way of decompressing from the day," that's different – it's a conscious choice, and it allows you to enjoy the activity because you've fit it into the overall fabric of your day. The weekly "cheat meal" can be enjoyed when it's part of an overall plan – one brick in the house – as opposed to, "Damn it, I spontaneously went to McDonald's because I'm a weak idiot, and since I'm those things anyway, I might as well go again tomorrow."

Constructive time doesn't mean *doing* the way we normally think of it. Just like watching the soap opera or going to the burger joint, watching the grass grow can be a specific, conscious, healthy element of your daily practice. (Lying in the grass can be a beautiful thing. Especially on your back, looking up at the sky, spotting shapes in the clouds and listening to the birds.) A planned power nap is constructive time. Nodding off randomly throughout the day because you're exhausted is not. One is part of an approach; one happens arbitrarily. The first allows you to refresh and recharge; the second adds to a feeling of laziness and lethargy. In the first scenario, you come away saying, "I'm ready to get back at it." In the second, you say, "There's an hour I'll never get back."

Riding the Waves

Even when you're practicing good habits, things come up that put a fly in the ointment (or a hitch in the plan, or a wrench in the works – whatever you prefer). I like to think of this in terms of surfing. (I haven't attempted the sport myself, though I like the analogy.) You paddle out, seek a good wave, lift yourself up, and ride. It takes energy, confidence, balance and stamina.

Of course, eventually you're going to lose that wave, either by getting knocked off it or from its natural break. In the same way, life is inevitably going to throw some unpredictable stuff your way. The same way we're advised to budget ten percent of our annual income for unanticipated house repairs, there's a certain degree of volatility that will occur in life in every period, and when they happen and toss you off the board and into the water, you need to get back on the board. Embedding consistent habits is like surfing. No matter how great a certain wave may be, it will break at some point, or you'll be thrown from the board, and your momentum will be interrupted. The thing that knocks you off the board or the wave breaking into shore are temporary interruptions that threaten to derail your consistency. Get back on the board. Paddle back out. Find your next wave. Heed the words of Australian actor and author F.M. Alexander: "People do not decide their futures, they decide their habits, and their habits decide their futures."

A Penny a Day

Sometimes you may feel like you just aren't getting there. Or anywhere. *I'm doing all these things I'm supposed to do,* you think to yourself, *I'm practicing these good habits every day – okay, almost every day – and it still isn't paying off. What gives?*

The thing is, it actually is paying off. Things are happening invisibly, and those different parts of the house are taking shape. It's just sometimes hard to recognize the structure coming together until it looks like a house. Though a series of beams, joists and pipes may not look like much, they are the essential parts of reaching the whole. All those expressions – good things come to those who wait, persistence pays off, etc. – they're all true, as much as we'd like them not to be. The good news is, the rewards feel great, and when you get them, you know you've earned them.

Quick question: If I offered you a million dollars right now or one cent that would double every day for thirty days, which would you choose?

Did you choose the million dollars? (You may have heard this story before and know the right answer, yet still reflexively chose the million.) If you did, you left millions more on the table. If you chose to receive the penny today, tomorrow it would be worth, of course, two cents. The next day, four cents, the day after that, eight, at which point you'd be saying, thanks a lot, Chad, fat lot of good I can do with eight measly cents.

Of course, if you were to wait another four days, that single penny would be worth $1.28 – and you'd still be questioning your association with me. By day twelve, when the penny had passed the twenty-dollar mark, you might be starting to think I'm not so crazy (at least not based on this). Six days after that, your humble cent would have grown well past a cool thousand. And by day twenty-eight, that thousand will have been left in the dust and you'd be looking at six zeros. At the end of the thirty days, you'd be wondering how to spend $5,368,709.

This principle has a direct parallel to all those daily habits and behaviors you're putting in place. Individually, they're helping you use your hours more productively and efficiently. Together, they are making your time more constructive and paving a path toward powerful results. Though sometimes these results will seem to happen overnight, they reflect the combined effect of positive habits applied consistently over time. Look for ways to make those habits immutable parts of your day. Do the work, acknowledge your progress, push through the inevitable blips, and watch the house come together.

Jeremy's Story

When I was younger, I weighed on average about 190 pounds – maybe 180 at my fittest. I was exercising every day, eating well, getting good rest.

In 2008, soon after I closed a sale on a home, the new owners discovered termite damage, and launched a lawsuit against my firm. The case ended up lasting over four years. At first, my company was found guilty on several counts. The case then went to Texas Appellate Court, who overturned the original verdict. The buyers weren't satisfied. They took it all the way to the Supreme Court, who thankfully agreed with the Appellate Court's ruling.

So we were vindicated in the end, however it would be a lie to say that period didn't take a serious toll on me. My wife was dragged through the case. I lost a friend to brain cancer, as well as the first agent I worked with, to colon cancer. A colleague died of a heart attack, and I witnessed his final moments. Worst of all, my mentor, who owned the office, died of leukemia. All of this happened before the charges were eventually overturned.

During all that time, I turned to food to cope with the constant stress. I didn't realize it while I was doing it, and it caught up with me. It doesn't take very long to get out of shape. Before I knew it, I'd gained a hundred pounds.

From the outside, things looked okay. I was still meeting my professional goals and taking care of everyone else. The issue is that I'd stopped taking care of myself. Along with the reckless eating came plenty of drinking, not exercising, and throwing myself into work to an unreasonable degree as a means of distraction from all the tension and difficulty. I was on a dangerous path.

I decided I needed to change something, make a meaningful shift in some context of my life. In 2017, I decided it was time to take the leap and go out on my own as a business and life coach. People's reactions ranged from subtly skeptical to overtly negative. Some questioned me, saying things like, "You have it good here, why risk it?" Without the safety net of the company, they doubted I could succeed.

From my existing network, maybe ten people signed up to become clients, which felt like a promising start. For the first couple of years, it stayed primarily those ten. Then, starting with the third year or so, I started getting other clients through word of mouth. I started entrenching consistent habits into my day with the goal of doing whatever I could to initiate and nurture relationships. I also took the key step of closing my real estate license so people in the industry wouldn't see me as a threat. These things in combination helped expand my business more and more. Soon I was able to expand my business to other cities throughout Texas, and as far as Arkansas. It continues growing today.

This professional journey showed me that I have the courage and resilience to make change. In this case, it was taking a risk by closing one career door to open another. It's taken strict intent and, as I said, the building of consistent habits, along with ongoing support from my family and friends.

Having experienced successful change in a professional context, I felt the confidence to apply those same principles to me as a person – specifically, to my drastic weight gain. The tipping point for this was an evening when I was out with a close friend, who very directly said, "Jer, I've seen you at your best. Now I'm seeing you at your worst." He showed me a video about intermittent fasting, then gave me a contact name who represented a popular fitness program.

I'm a kinesiology major by study, though not by practice, and was interested in the science of weight loss and proper nutrition, which I obviously hadn't been practicing. I took a chance on the program. When the people there looked at me and explained the rigor and discipline necessary to succeed, I saw in their eyes some of the same skepticism I'd seen in my colleagues hearing me announce I was launching my own business.

The program was challenging to say the least. This wasn't just intermittent fasting. It involved fasts of up to forty-eight hours and frequently doing OMAD, or One Meal A Day. Though I was intimidated, I was also confident. I was committed to translating that professional transformation into a personal one.

They call the first week hell week. It consists of three forty-eight-hour fasts separated by one meal. Somehow, I got through it. Then there are consecutive fasts of seventy-two and forty-eight hours separated by a single meal. I somehow got through those, too. The weight started coming off. In a fairly short time, OMADs became easy.

I liked the direct approach and the tough love they gave me, just as my friend had. I respond to that. They told me, look, if you're not going to do it, don't bother wasting our time and your money. Accountability within the group helps, too. I attend a couple of meetings each week – hearing success stories from others keeps me believing I can do this – and chat with a mindset coach every Sunday to keep me mentally focused on my goals. So far I've lost forty pounds in about twelve weeks. My ultimate goal is to lose one hundred. I know now that I'll get there.

There's a common factor between growing the practice and losing the weight. It isn't setting the goal, though that's obviously important. It's embedding the habits that allow you to meet it. To me, it's about reverse-engineering the process. You have an end zone you're aiming for, whatever that may specifically represent in your life, and you need to figure out the plays that will get you there, the acts that will get you down the field, the small daily choices that will get you closer to the finish line. You need to do those activities every day, with as much consistency as possible. No one is going to maintain one hundred percent good habits one hundred percent of the time, and they may not be natural or instinctive habits to you. On some days, even when you are practicing those good habits, you may not see results. Stick with it. Over time, they come.

Chapter 15: W1N One Day At A Time

In the last chapter, we talked about the concept of building good habits and embedding them so that these behaviors become, after a while, automatic, or at least nearly so. We discussed what it means to use your hours well, meaning (a) productively and (b) efficiently, and how accomplishing both these aims results in what I call constructive time. The more constructive time you engage in, the more you build toward pursuit of your apex.

Allow me to shift from conceptual to practical. Specifically, let's look at a tool I developed for the purpose of setting, and meeting, daily goals in order to ultimately meet bigger ones, called W1N (said as "Win 1"), or, in full, W1N One Day at a Time. It's proved a powerful facilitator for many of my clients, and I want to share it with you in the hope that it can likewise help you explore your best possible you.

Asking What Matters

At a certain point in my life and career, I found myself getting too busy, less organized, more scattered, and not as productive as I felt I needed to be if I were going to be successful for myself and others. I did a brainstorming session to find a tool that would help me focus on the things that mattered most in my world and therefore contribute most to achieving my apex. My thinking was that, if I could identify priority areas and do at least one thing every day to seed each of them, I could count it as a good day – a productive day – and that, if I continued this pattern consistently enough, I would see cumulative results over time.

In the last chapter and others, we've talked about focusing on the process, which you can control, rather than the outcome, which you can't. This tool was intended to take that guiding principle and translate it into something concrete. For example, we've all heard repeatedly that when you start to exercise regularly and eat better, you may not see an overnight transformation on the scale, however by sticking with those committed behaviors, you'll experience different types of wins along that journey – your clothes fitting differently, your skin looking better, others starting to comment. This tool was intended as a forcing mechanism to keep me focused on daily actions and behaviors so that I could sleep well each night knowing I'd put in the effort that day and moved another step in the right direction. I'd trust that the results would come. It would also – and this is paramount – help me focus on the things that I got done that day instead of tossing and turning all night feeling guilty about what I didn't.

I identified four crucial areas to serve each day, with a view toward producing meaningful results over time. These four areas were Love, Improvement, Fitness, and Economics – which became the acronym LIFE.

Once I began engaging in this practice of doing at least one thing every day to serve each priority category, it led to positive new results. This evolved into the W1N tool, the concept being that contributing to these areas every day meant winning that day, and by winning one day at a time, one will start to see the overall needle move. Again, instead of stressing about the hours I may have felt I didn't use well on a certain day, or worrying about the abstract distance I felt I stood from specific goals, I stayed focused on the concrete things I had done each day and the energy I'd put forth in service of each priority area.

Once I felt the tool was helping me in a sustained way, I introduced it to some of my clients. For some, it helped them pause and think about the true priority areas in their lives, just as it had for me. We're all busy, and often we go through the motions of each day without thinking about whether what we're doing is really what matters, or what we want to be doing, or what will allow us to move in the direction we desire. For others, it provided a certain amount of structure and clarity simply by helping them organize the days consistently and then entrench particular behaviors. The most gratifying outcome was that, after some months, many people started telling me how the tool had helped them strengthen their relationships, realize personal growth, improve their health, and take control of their finances.

Making the Calendar Your Boss

In the previous chapter, we talked about using your hours well. Now let's talk about a way to put those hours into a tangible framework that you can set up consistently and execute daily. Here's the good news. You're already familiar with this framework. It's called your calendar!

A big reason, maybe the biggest reason, we deviate from all our well-intended plans is our natural human emotionality, impulsivity and irrationality. Don't punish yourself for exhibiting these traits. We all have them, and we all let them get the better of us more often than we'd like to admit. Knowing this, it stands to reason that the more you can remove those potential obstacles from your decision-making throughout the day, the more likely you are to stick to your plans and hit your goals.

I applied this thinking to my overall calendar similarly to the way I'd identified the four priority areas. It isn't just young kids who benefit from routine, after all. Apex achievers have routines that include the start of their day, the end of it, and everything in between. The more consistent our rhythms, the more primed we are to perform at a high level in a consistent way.

The goal of optimizing my overall calendar led me to divide each day into five categories and allot a specific amount of time for each. (New acronym alert!) Those five categories ended up as the non-negotiable ways I'd fill the SPACE in my calendar every day.

In other words:

First, the Start of the day. This comes down to a simple question: When will you wake up every day? The more consistent you can make it, the better. Taking this a step further, establishing a consistent routine after waking up is also beneficial, especially for the purpose of making sure you activate yourself, as opposed to just getting up, getting dressed and immediately sitting down in a chair to start working, or driving to an office and doing so. That's just getting up to get back down. One person I know does fifty pushups as his unchanging first act after getting out of bed. Another takes a shower, gets dressed, then walks a one-mile circle around the neighborhood to get her blood pumping. A third prepares a coffee then reads for thirty minutes to build general knowledge and awareness. For some people I know, starting the day right warrants ten minutes; for others, an hour. You decide what's optimal for you.

Next, the Promises on your calendar. These are the obligations, responsibilities and commitments which are unmovable (or at least shouldn't be moved since they affect others): the haircut you've booked; your son's dentist appointment; your daughter's soccer game; the gym class you take; date night with your spouse; the meeting with your client. Promises are fixed items over which you have no control. Sometimes they're one-offs, sometimes they repeat. They're there, you know exactly what they are, where you need to be, and how much of your time is required. Some people will have many of these in a given week that take up a significant number of hours; others will have few.

Third, the things you aim to do for **A**dvancement in the four LIFE priority areas – Love, Improvement, Fitness, Economics – by doing at least one thing every day to nurture them.

Fourth, designated **C**haos time – for the unanticipated and unforeseeable things that occur during the day. Though you may not be able to predict what they are, or when they're going to show up, you can reserve time to deal with them. There are two types of chaos events: controllable and uncontrollable. An example of the former is someone texting to ask if you have fifteen minutes to chat – you can politely (or, in my case, directly) say you don't, and you can connect with them during the Chaos block. An example of the latter is a flat tire – you have to deal with it then and there. Chaos events threaten to offset the rest of the calendar. When you book time for them in advance, you can shift other things around as necessary and prevent the whole from getting torpedoed.

Finally, and most important of all (even though it's the last letter in the acronym), the **E**nd of the day, and another simple question: When will you go to bed? Most people have a harder time ending the day at a consistent time than they do starting it that way. If you can't make it the same time every night, at minimum have a consistent schedule, with no more than two different bedtimes during the week. I won't be the first person you've heard say how important sleep is, both physically and mentally. Give yourself the vital gift of rest. Don't stay on your phone or watch TV until the moment you lay down your head. Take a bath. Do some light exercise or active breathing. Read poetry. Then drift away, enjoy your dreams, and get ready to wake up refreshed and ready for all the wonderful possibilities the following day will bring!

Note: By fixing the times for both the start and end of your day, you're doing the most basic, and most essential, things to foster your health. Proper rest helps restore your energy, clarity and focus and propels you up the mountain toward your apex. You have just one body – treat it like the temple it is! Also, when you establish consistent start and end times, you're already managing about one third of the twenty-four hours in your calendar.

Making the calendar your boss is empowering and liberating at the same time. It's up to you to do the work up front, figuring out your

SPACE components, when and where they should be placed, and how much time each one merits.

Here are two other important suggestions.

First, build your weekly calendar on Sundays, which allows you to use logic more than emotion (since logic and emotion are basically opposites).

Second, make the important distinction between regular and recurring events. The former are those which you commit to doing on a consistent basis, yet whose timing may be affected by other factors. The latter are locked in and not subject to change by outside influences. These recurring events can therefore be entered on auto-repeat. Regular items, on the other hand, should be entered individually. Taking your kids to school happens at the same time every day. You can't decide to move it back two hours. Exercising may be something you're also dedicated to doing every day, though you may not always be able to do it at the same time because outside factors may affect this decision. Since no two days are the same, and individual items may be affected by what's happening around them during a given week or on a particular day, it's most effective for you to construct each week fresh, apart from those items that are truly unchangeable. Taking the time to place all other items on the calendar individually gives them the weight they deserve, and starts you off on the proper foot.

Once you're done populating your calendar, you ask it what you need to do every day, then do it. Why does this work? Three reasons:

▲ Your day is like a puzzle. You need all the pieces to be able to complete it and see that satisfyingly complete picture. When life's quirks happen, it can be like one of those pieces being bumped and knocked off the edge of the table, throwing everything else out of whack and leaving the puzzle frustratingly incomplete. When you have the pieces laid out ahead of time, it's like putting a fence around them – even though they may shift and slide, you won't lose any. You can still finish the puzzle, even if not necessarily in the way you envisioned.

▲ The more parts of your day you have scheduled and blocked out, the less stress you'll experience, and the less likelihood of filling the white space with counterproductive activity. White space on your calendar will tend to get filled up with the white noise of life. As I've said in earlier chapters, "counterproductive" is not the same as "doing nothing," which can be healthy and restorative. Schedule that active downtime – as "me time," "creative time," "watching a bad rom-com time," whatever. That way it can be blocked out, and the details can still be spontaneous.

▲ Doing this SPACE exercise will, after a short period, likely highlight tendencies you didn't observe before. You'll see which parts are consistently easy for you to do, which are consistently hard, and which vary. When you miss one workout in a week because you offered to help your cousin move, that's an isolated event. When you miss two because you felt too tired at the time the workout was scheduled, that alerts you to the need to shift things around in the calendar. When you miss three, the issue is probably beyond the calendar.

Winning at LIFE

Let's return to the A in SPACE – **A**dvancement – which is about the four areas of LIFE I encourage you to foster each day. Nurturing the four priorities contributes to winning the day. And every day you win is another step in pursuit of your apex.

Real-life examples for me in the four areas include: in my love life, communicating in my wife Nita's love languages, which for her largely involves time and touch; for improvement, I commit thirty minutes per day to reading or listening to a podcast with a focus on growth; for fitness, drinking a gallon of water each day, exercising, and tracking my food so I'm aware of the choice I make; and for economics, reviewing my budget and expenses every month. (You may remember my mentioning earlier that my natural organizational skills are not exactly superb. Okay, they suck.)

The way you choose to address these priority areas shouldn't be subject to daily change. Cultivate them the way you would tend a garden over a season. Pay attention to it by watering the soil, ensuring adequate sunlight, fertilizing, and pruning, while the plants remain. This, too, is a seasonal exercise. Identify overarching priorities you want to nurture the same way you would your garden, for at least a few months. Once you've made progress, you may want to keep growing those same plants, or maybe put in some new ones to tend and watch blossom. Maintain this cycle, making yourself the metaphorical garden and watching new habits bloom as you make your way ever forward.

At the end of every day, Nita and I ask each other what the best part was. We do this for a few reasons. First, as I mentioned earlier, it helps us both focus on the parts of the day we feel we won, instead of regretting those we didn't. Second, it puts us in a positive frame of mind before falling asleep, instead of allowing in any stress or tension due to outside stuff. Finally, it reminds us every night, as we lie in bed together and prepare to fall asleep, that in every day there is at least one positive moment to share and celebrate.

After all, slow and steady wins the race. The W1N tool is all about encouraging that steady, consistent progress over time. As I've said in other parts of the book and with reference to other principles or tools, you don't need to aim for one hundred percent. Not only do the broad seasons of your life change, requiring you to focus on different aspects of yourself and your growth; things also happen in your day-to-day that will sometimes prevent ticking those intended boxes. A relationship change causes you to nurture your love goals differently. Mastering one area of self-improvement motivates you to challenge yourself with another. An injury necessitates an adjustment of your fitness goals. A career change is accompanied by a shift in your finances.

No matter the ongoing changes in the way you structure your calendar and address your LIFE priorities, the guiding principle holds: win one day at a time. And keep on climbing toward your apex.

Tiffany's Story

I was a single mom going through a divorce when I felt I needed to make a change. I'd always had a hard time knowing what fulfilled me or defining meaningful life goals. My strength was in executing tasks; my weakness, in understanding what it was I really wanted to achieve. My divorce increased my expenses, so I needed to get a second job. At the same time, I met Chad and invested in his coaching based on a recommendation from a business associate of mine, who suggested it would benefit me to have someone in my corner helping me define more concrete objectives.

He was right. Being forced to define one's goals makes it easier to achieve them. It sounds so obvious, yet so many of us don't take the time to do it. I don't feel I'm super creative, so I do better when someone pushes me to articulate my objectives and determine the necessary steps to make them a reality.

The W1N system was a great fit for me because, as I said, once I have a structure to work with, execution comes naturally. The process is nice and clear: Win each day to win the week. Win each week to win the month. Win each month to win the year. When I feel anxious or overwhelmed, the framework helps serve as a mental and psychological anchor. It gives structure to each day, which both calms me and helps me get focused.

The four categories within the LIFE acronym – Love, Improvement, Fitness, Economics – are all areas where I knew I could improve. Having a specific list of things to achieve in each category every day gives me a clear picture of what I'm doing to meet my bigger goals. As an example, in the category of Love, I make sure I take the time to tell both my daughter and my fiancé two positive things every day. That small reminder helps me be more present and intentional with the two people who mean the most to me. For self-improvement, I do something every day to nourish my spirit, like reading, or watching something that makes me laugh. For fitness, it's fueling my body with the right food and exercising daily. For economics, it's spending a certain amount of time each day on lead generation.

I don't always meet the goals. When I fail to tick certain boxes, my coach and I talk about what happened and why, and if it's necessary to adjust the plan or my approach to it. Then I jump right back in. The key to it, the part that isn't adjustable, is accountability. If I'm accountable to my coach, then I'm being accountable to myself. I've doubled my business every year for the past three. I look forward to teaching the system to my teenage daughter so she can use it to give structure to her life and achieve her own goals.

Chapter 16: Value Footprints

Winning the day isn't always so simple. Things get in the way. You can have strong intentions, establish a clear vision, remain firm in your self-belief. Then you step on a loose rock during your ascent; or you start to make headway toward your goal only to run into an obstacle around the corner; or you march forward steadily, consistent in your progress, focused on your destination, before discovering that your bearings are off.

Whatever you aim to do, whatever peak you want to reach, there is a trail for you to take. Your road may be the precise one someone has taken before, or it may reflect the fact that no one has. Both contain equal possibility.

Following Others' Footsteps

Have others laid the path for what you hope to achieve? Sometimes, the smartest choice is to replicate exactly what someone else has already done. The trail to success doesn't always require change or innovation; it can come down to faithfully executing a reliable template. You need to decide where your energy, thinking and resources are best placed. If a proven model for meeting your objective exists, it only makes sense to follow it.

Long before GPS arrived, sailors would faithfully use Polaris, the North Star, as their guide because of its unchanging position in the night sky. By measuring the angle between the northern horizon and the star, they could accurately determine latitude, and therefore steer with greater assurance toward their intended destination. Unmistakably and unvaryingly, this mystical point of light for centuries provided navigators a proven guide to help them continue on in search of their goal.

Those of us who have lived in a northern climate know that, when you cross-country ski, you follow tracks already in the snow, made by those who were already there. You know the tracks are reliable, and that they will lead you to your destination. You need not do any work to figure out the route or lay down the steps. You just need to concentrate on following them (and not falling down. Cross-country skiing is harder than it looks, at least for me.) Cyclists often "draft" off the competitor ahead of them, positioning themselves within the slipstream to take advantage of the energy exerted by the other person while conserving their own. In the skiing example, the tracks have been laid by others hours before. In the cycling one, the course is being charted by someone else at the same moment. In both scenarios, the best choice is to follow.

Why do so many singers release Christmas albums? Because there's no more dependable template for selling albums. Fans have shown that they will buy the same collections of yuletide songs over and over. Why not follow such a successful model? Why are certain movies remade over and over (and why do I keep watching each new *Halloween* installment even though it scares the bejeezus out of me)? Because the prototype has proven itself, and the most sensible path to success is duplication.

Such blueprints can be so successful that people resist changes to them. Think of your reaction when you go to a concert and the band or artist puts a new spin on a particular tune. You're probably somewhat miffed, because you want to hear the song exactly as you know and love it. You want to sing every line, anticipate each pause, appreciate that key change near the end, and do the air guitar and drum solos exactly as they are supposed to be, with no messing around. If the model has produced consistent results, sometimes the best thing to do is stay loyal to it and sing the song just as it is.

Here are three principles to keep in mind before you embark on a known path:

- ⋏ *Choose footprints you know you can follow.* Don't aim for ones so big that your steps are the wrong fit, or those so far ahead that they'll melt by the time you get there. Seek those for which your current strides are the right match.

- ⋏ *Study the path.* Before you take the first step, make sure you know where it leads, how long it is, and if it's one continuous route or divided into sections or part of a larger network. Understand as much about the journey as you can before starting down it.

- ⋏ *Don't follow blindly.* A path isn't necessarily worth following just because it's there. Some loop back on themselves endlessly, some stop abruptly, some lead to undesirable destinations. Learn everything you can about it, then take time to think and reflect before taking the leap.

Adapting the Route

Perhaps tracks have been laid that are nearly the ones you need, though not quite in the same context as yours or according to quite the same parameters. These are tracks you use as a guide, adapting them as necessary, re-adjusting as you go. While we often hear about "brand new" innovations, "game-changing" inventions or "revolutionary" approaches, the truth is that most innovation and invention happens slowly, in tiny augmentations, through zig-zag paths. As Thomas Edison said, "I have not failed. I've just found ten thousand ways that won't work."

Elite sprinters, skiers and swimmers spend years seeking ways to shave hundredths of seconds off their times by exploring tiny modifications in strategy, equipment or technique. The International Amateur Athletics Federation began recognizing records in the men's one-hundred-meter sprint in 1912, starting with 10.6 seconds. In 1936, the record was brought down to 10.2 by the famous Jesse Owens, and though many would go on to match his time in the subsequent two decades, it would be that long before anyone found a way to go faster – by only another tenth of a second.

By the early 1960s, with improvements seeming less and less likely and many experts starting to assert that humans simply couldn't run any faster and we'd reached the limits of human achievement in this particular pursuit, the record was now being measured in hundredths, rather than tenths, of a second.

Of course, virtually every time someone expresses a belief that we've reached a certain limit, we tend to find a way to break through it. In 1968, American sprinter Jim Hines won the hundred-meter in a blazing 9.95 seconds. After that, it would take another fourteen years for the record to be improved upon – by two more hundredths of a second, to 9.93. Improvement can take time even when the footprints are well established. Here's another one from Edison, a little more direct this time: "There's a way to do it better – find it."

Staking Your Own Path

When there's no precedent for your vision, when what you have in mind is distinct from everything that's come before, well, that's when you've got yourself a brand new snowfall just waiting for fresh prints. Your only guide is a beautiful blank canvas, and it's the moment to take your shot at doing something in a way that hasn't been done. You might stumble – maybe more than once. You might also create new possibilities or shatter barriers no one thought possible.

Above, we talked about the hundred-meter sprint record being set in 1968 and standing for fifteen years before being lowered by a mere two-hundredths of a second. At that point, in 1983, the experts who in the Sixties had expressed skepticism that humans could run any faster were now saying it was *really* unlikely that we could go any faster. Still the winning times continued to drop, in ever-slighter increments, as runners, coaches, trainers and biomechanical scientists seeking innovations in movement, technique and strategy to get lower and winners sometimes needing to be measured using specialized photo imagery.

Then along came the Jamaican sprinter Usain Bolt, built unlike traditional sprinters, casual and extroverted at the start of races, with a loose upper-body running style seen as non-fundamental (since a certain way of doing anything is clung to as "fundamental" only until it is improved upon). His example was one of literally establishing new footprints: Taller than most of his competitors, he would take about forty-one strides over the course of the race, whereas almost all others took about forty-five. Though Bolt was in one sense running the same race as the others, in another, he was running his own.

By 2006, the record had been lowered to 9.77 seconds. In 2007, Bolt ran a 9.74 in Italy. The following year, he ran 9.72 at a competition in New York. Two and a half months after that, Usain, now known as the "Lighting Bolt", went 9.69 at the Olympic Games in Beijing, becoming the first person to break the hardly imagined 9.7 barrier. And exactly a year after that, at the World Championships in Berlin – in the same stadium where Jesse Owens had set the record seventy-three years earlier – he did the unthinkable, shattering his own mark by more than a full tenth of a second, running the race in 9.58 seconds.

While it's the slow, marginal improvements that are more common, Bolt-like leaps regularly occur throughout history, by those who dare to do something in a new or different way despite the doubts or fears of others or opposition to something being done non-traditionally, non-fundamentally, or non-acceptably.

There are no limits to how high you can aim, how far you can go, or in which direction you can dream. Think about Sir Edmund Hillary and Tenzing Norgay summiting Mount Everest in 1953. Ferdinand Magellan starting the expedition that resulted in the first circumnavigation of the globe in 1522. (He died partway through the journey in the Philippines and it was finished by his shipmates.) Jacques Cousteau inventing the aqualung in 1943 to allow divers to first explore beyond depths of a hundred feet, paving the way for others to eventually plumb the very ocean floor.

None of these monumental achievements happened quickly or easily. Staking your own path often means making multiple starts, adjusting course, and redoubling your efforts. You take those first steps, start to feel progress, and down comes another snowfall, making the field again an endless sheet of white. Keep going and embrace the journey.

Emulating Hero Traits

Just as there is always a path waiting for you to take the first step – by following established footprints, adapting the route to your situation, or charting your own course – there are valuable models to be found in the behaviors and traits displayed by those around you and others who have come before.

Here's a valuable exercise. Take a blank sheet of paper. On it, list people you consider heroes. This might include parents or other family members, teachers you've had, athletes you admire, historical figures, spiritual leaders, standouts in your professional field, and so on. Make the list as long as you'd like. Mine, for example, contains names such as Jackie Robinson, my childhood hero, John C. Maxwell, a business leader I hold in high esteem, and my wife, the anchor to my energy and spirit.

Now, beside each name, list the attributes you feel make each individual heroic. Then, of all the attributes you've written down, circle the dozen that resonate most with you.

Take another sheet of paper. Take the twelve attributes you circled from the other page and rank them, from those you're most challenged by to those in which you feel you're strongest. (Remember, we develop strengths and leverage weaknesses.)

Each number now matches a month of the year. The attribute you ranked first, meaning the one you find you're most challenged by, is going to be your focus for the following January. The second attribute is the one you'll pay special attention to in February. And so on. Continue to broaden yourself one attribute one at a time – by reading books, watching videos, observing others, requesting conversations – and then look back at the end of the year to appreciate the changes you've made. By taking a month to focus on one heroic attribute at a time, you will more closely resemble your heroes by the end of next year. Capes and tights are optional.

Whether you're choosing to repeat a path in exactly the way someone else has, improving on an established route by taking it in a different way, or establishing fresh prints where no others have tread, do it in a way that is sincerely and authentically you. Even if you're wearing an outfit made popular by someone else, it's still you inside it. Even if you're wearing the same shoes as someone else who reached a certain destination, it's still you who must take the steps. Honor the guides whose paths you follow and stay true to yourself as you pursue your own apex, participating in the unstoppable human instinct to forge unknown paths and seek new horizons. In other words – if you don't mind one final Edison quote – "I start where the last man left off."

Courtney's Story

From a young age growing up in Cedar Grove, New Jersey, I was a real tomboy. I was naturally big and strong. I liked sports. I'd participate in races with my brother and his football teammates – and I'd win.

I was also, among my four brothers and one sister, the one with an identity issue. The boys in my grade didn't know what to make of a girl who was big, strong and athletic, and the girls didn't hang out with me because they saw me as more of a boy. So I didn't fit in with anyone.

When I was twelve, I tried to go into modeling. Since I already felt successful in sports, I thought it might be a good complement. Plus, I still wanted to feel feminine and wear dresses and get my nails done. None of the agencies were interested in me because of my athletic body type. They told me I'd never be accepted.

I stayed focused on sports throughout my teen years, playing basketball, football and soccer, as well as running track. I even skipped my high school prom for a basketball game. I ended up earning a scholarship to play basketball at the University of Scranton. There, I continued to excel as an athlete, and, more important, started to feel more comfortable in my own skin. In that environment, my strength and athleticism were more than accepted; they were celebrated. I felt like I was becoming the best version of myself. However, it was a feeling that came to an abrupt halt when I graduated and had to enter the real world. I felt lost. Sports had always been both my safety net and the thing that allowed me to feel successful. Suddenly, it wasn't either of those.

After kind of drifting for a while and figuring out who I was and, once again, where I belonged, I discovered the right gym and was hooked immediately. I loved the challenge, I loved the feeling, and I especially loved the community – people of all shapes and sizes supporting each other. When you pick up a barbell, it isn't about where you come from, what you believe in, or what you look like. It's about the common goal of getting the most out of yourself. No one commented on whether I was big or small, and no one described me as "strong for a woman" – they just described me as strong. Like back in college, I was being celebrated for just being me.

I ended up not only competing in CrossFit; I also became a coach. At twenty-nine, I quit my corporate job in the mortgage field to become a full-time CrossFit coach and open my own personal training business, with the goal of helping others become the best version of themselves, too. I called it Iron Grace.

At the same time, I decided to make another go at modeling. I felt more confident in myself, and physiques like mine seemed to be gaining more acceptance. I sent portfolios to dozens of agencies, and, like before, got rejected by all of them. One particularly direct guy told me, "No little girl is going to want to look like you." Though it didn't affect me as harshly as it had when I was twelve, I gave up on it for a second time.

Some months later, my mom, while at the US Open tennis tournament, ended up by chance sitting next to the assistant editor of Vogue, who said she was scouting for fitness models. My mom showed her pictures and videos of me. To make a long story short, a week later the woman called me asking me to visit their offices in New York. They asked, "What separates you as a fitness model?" I said, "I'm not trying to be a fitness model. I'm just trying to be myself." They signed me on the spot. At one point, I was sent to replace a boxer for a photo shoot in a warehouse in Brooklyn. A few weeks later, on my thirtieth birthday, I saw the current issue of Vogue on the newsstand, with a multi-page spread of me from that shoot. That opened the floodgates – people became eager to promote me and endorse my message of female strength and body-positivity.

The following year, the WWE – World Wrestling Entertainment – reached out to me to ask if I was interested in becoming one of their "Divas." Though that didn't work out, while I was at the tryouts in Orlando, I met a couple of past contestants from The Titan Games, who convinced me to submit an application. I did, and a month later got a call from them saying they wanted to do a FaceTime interview with me to show Dwayne "The Rock" Johnson, the show's host. I had a mini heart attack while saying yes. After interviewing with a couple producers, I was invited to participate in the combine, which was one of the best parts of the experience. One of the workouts was a max deadlift. Between the cheering, the awareness that The Rock was secretly watching, and the adrenaline pumping through me, I hit a personal best. A week later, they called and told me to pack my bags because I was leaving for Atlanta and couldn't tell anyone where I was going or why.

On the show, I went on to win the Titan Games, Eastern Division, and earned the title The Beast of the East. That gave me more visibility and a broader platform. I've since expanded my business to include motivational speaking and a clothing fitness line. I want to keep motivating people and spreading the word about being healthy and strong, and accepting yourself and others for who they are, through my tagline, *Be Strong, Live Confident*. Throughout my life, I've gone against the odds and was often met with skepticism or outright rejection. I stayed true to who I was and bet on myself at every stage, which ultimately paid off. My goal now is to help others find the strongest and most authentic version of themselves, and to let them know that what makes us strong is the moments of weakness we overcome, and that we find the light in ourselves by getting through the moments of darkness. When people tell you they don't see the box you fit into, redefine the box.

Chapter 17: Respect the Plus/Minus

We're driven to succeed. We seek visibility and recognition. We have pride, we like accolades, we want others to respond to what we're saying, writing, selling, teaching. We strive passionately toward our goals, resolved to knock aside every obstacle that gets in the way.

The more absorbed we become in pursuit of our personal apex, the greater the potential for us to develop tunnel vision that keeps us focused more and more on ourselves and less and less on those around us. Neglecting the power of others, however – how you can help them, and how they can help you – means squandering opportunities to produce greater results than anyone could achieve on their own.

As you quest forward in pursuit of your zenith, remember that one of your greatest strengths lies in the ability to help others, and your willingness to let them help you. Or, in the words of the famous American novelist Edith Wharton, "There are two ways of spreading light: to be the candle or the mirror that reflects it."

Giving Help

Some sports use a boatload of statistics to assess performance. Baseball in particular, especially in today's world of sabermetrics and "advanced stats," cuts and slices its numbers in countless ways to evaluate players, give fodder to commentators, and spark barroom arguments. Hockey (I know, another hockey analogy), on the other hand, still uses relatively few measures, at least compared to other sports. Goals and assists are, as they have been since the game began, the two most cited.

My favorite hockey statistic, however, is the "plus/minus," a figure as simple as it is revealing: how many goals a player's team scores while he's on the ice versus the number of goals the opponents score while he's on. This formula provides an easy glimpse of overall value, and reflects the many ways in which a player can contribute to the shared outcome that are less concrete or obvious than scoring goals. I like plus/minus because it can't lie. If the team is scoring a lot when you're playing, that says something unmistakable, whether or not it's your name showing up most often on the scoresheet.

My second-favorite statistic in hockey is the assist, especially because, for every goal scored, up to two assists, rather than just one, are recorded. This is acknowledgement that the end result we see often starts well before, with one player putting in motion a positive sequence of events by acting as a catalyst for the next player. The goal we ultimately witness might look effortless. More often than not, it's the culmination of a series of cooperative actions.

Every so often, there is a spectacular individual effort that results in a goal. Look at the box score for a typical game, however, and you'll see very few "unassisted" goals. As a fan, ask yourself this: When you watch replays, do you pay more attention to that last moment when the puck goes in the net, or to the sequence that led up to it?

Do you ever watch Olympic rowing? There are two types: sweep rowing, in which each rower has a single oar on opposite sides of the boat, and sculling, in which each rower has two oars. In both styles, whether in pairs, fours or eights, the success of the rowers has partially to do with their strength, partially to do with their stamina, though mostly to do with their synchronization – the assistance they give to the boat's motion with each combined and coordinated stroke. The more rowers there are assisting each other and the greater the harmony among their movements, the more speed they produce. A pair is faster than a single, a quad faster than a pair, an eight faster than a quad.

Similarly, while we're often astounded by how fast professional sprinters can run individually (in the previous chapter, we talked about Usain Bolt and others), consider how much faster they go when assisting each other. The individual record for the 400-meter dash is 43.03 seconds; for the 4x100-meter relay, it's 36.84. By executing all the subtle moments of assistance as precisely as possible – exchanging the baton in just the right way, ensuring just the right hand position, one runner accelerating at just the right rate as the other slows down – four people, in just one circuit of the track, can run nearly seven seconds faster than one person doing it alone.

Is it the fastest runner of the four who is always placed on the anchor leg? No. It's the coordination of effort, the way in which each person assists the other, that maximizes results. The fastest runner on the team may be best utilized for their quick start, skill on the turn, or ability to close. When all the members of a team apply their abilities in a way that contributes to the overall goal, amazing things can happen.

Did you ever play tug of war as a kid (or adult)? What a great sport: two sides pulling on a rope to see which one can win by dragging the other past a certain point. It seems so basic and primitive, yet it's the side that takes the sophisticated approach that always emerges victorious.

Do you remember debating whether to put the strongest person at the front or the back? And do you remember that, in the end, it didn't matter, because it was almost always the side that worked together best who won?

Just as in the relay, results are a function of how well the members of the team assist one another rather than the individual performance of each person. Perhaps you recall someone during a tug of war yelling, "Down, Pull! Down, Pull!" and then the thrill of finding a common tempo. The person who was yelling "Down, Pull!" is the same as the rowers' coxswain, responsible for coordinating the team's rhythm. Coxswains don't help power the boat – they don't even face the same way as the rowers – however they give commands that keep the race plan on track and the boat pointed toward its destination.

Have you ever been jumping on a trampoline with a friend, when one of you inadvertently bounces an instant earlier, suddenly launching the other much higher? This accidental boost is a classic demonstration of how powerful a small bit of assistance can be. In that fraction of a second, the first person transfers enough energy to the second to send them flying far higher than they could get using just their own force. A few days ago I was sent a video showing someone achieving what is claimed to be the first octuple trampoline somersault. Whether or not it's true, what compelled me most was watching the way the two others coordinated their joint bounces to occur just before those of the person attempting the record – and the way they all celebrated together, knowing he couldn't have accomplished it without the help of the others.

Nearly every "individual" success involves assistance by others. Though the goals scored are usually the most prominent part of what we witness, the assists are often the most valuable. In the previous chapter, we talked about Sir Edmund Hillary, who in the first years after that first ascent of Mount Everest received most of the credit and fame. However, without his Sherpa and companion Tenzing Norgay, who possessed critical knowledge of the mountain, Hillary would never have reached the celebrated summit or gained his everlasting glory.

When we talk about the value of assisting, in fact, there is no better example than that of climbers and their use of belaying, a process in which partners take turns controlling the ropes to help each other reach the desired heights. They're giving each other information through verbal communication, too, via brief statements such as "Slack," "Lowering" or "On me". Since they can't see each other on certain parts of a climb, the timing and precision of these commands is crucial. Sometimes, when it's hard to hear each other, they will communicate through a kind of Morse code via different ways of pulling on the ropes. Assistance can take many different forms, and it can be the vital difference in reaching the mountaintop.

The most significant benefit of assisting may be psychological. Studies show that helping others can reduce stress, improve mood, raise self-esteem, increase happiness, strengthen the immune system, promote a sense of belonging, broaden perspective…the list goes on. There is even evidence that it can increase life expectancy.

Getting Help

Just as it benefits you to help others, so should you be willing to receive help from them. There are so many reasons we often reject offers of assistance, all of them foolish. We want to do it all on our own. We feel no one else can do the job as well as we can, so there's no point in accepting. We're skeptical about others' motivations. We're concerned about someone stealing our thunder. We don't want to put them out.

Sure, sometimes flying solo has its place. Think of falcons, custom-built for going it alone, with their keen eyesight, lethal beaks, and unique aerodynamic design. (Peregrine falcons, the fastest species on Earth, have been recorded swooping at up to two hundred forty miles per hour.) We watch in awe as a lone hawk hovers above the treetops, scanning for a meal. These are creatures for whom individualism is an instinct and a superpower.

By contrast, think about the wonder you experience seeing the elegant perfection of a flock of ducks or geese in their signature V. Why do they fly in this formation? For efficiency. Each bird's airstream assists the one behind by helping reduce drag and increase lift. Throughout their flight, the birds rotate positions and coordinate flapping patterns to optimize the group's collective energy.

The V formation is a beautiful example of how powerful help can be. These birds continue assisting each other like this over sometimes thousands of miles. The strategy is so advantageous that we mimic it in everything from aerobatics shows to military flight formation.

There are countless ways in which we can provide help to one another – physical, mental, psychological, emotional, material, intellectual, spiritual. Keep striving toward your apex. Apply your individual skills and talents to their very maximum, while always remembering to give, and accept, help along the way.

David's Story

I grew up amid the cornfields of Iowa in a small town called Pella, population about ten thousand. Even though it felt to me like the middle of nowhere, and people there didn't exactly dream big, I decided at some point, for some reason, that I wanted to play in the NBA. I wasn't very tall, nor overly athletic. Nonetheless, that's what I set as my life's goal, and everything I did from that point on became a step toward it. My parents, god bless them, probably should have guided me toward baseball or golf, but they were unconditionally supportive, encouraging me to pursue my dream.

Coming from where I did, there was no template for reaching the professional ranks. I knew I was going to have to fight to reach my goal. I worked on my game every second I could, kept holding that dream firm in my mind. In my early teens, my family moved to Missouri for my dad's job as a window salesman, to a town called Kearney, which was even smaller than Pella. I kept pushing myself, improving as much as I could. In my last year of high school, I sent my highlight reel to schools across the country. My aim was to make it to a Division I program. No one from my high school had ever done that, and those around me didn't think I could. The frequent comment I heard was, "No one else has done it. How are you going to?" My mentality was, "Watch me be the first."

I was accepted by Western Illinois University, a Division I school. I spent three years there as a starter, the last two as captain. Though I played hard and practiced harder, I started to realize that my goal of making the NBA might be beyond my reach. I was only six-foot-two. Though I had squeezed every ounce out of my ability, I saw the talent (and size) of those around me and knew I had to be realistic. I adjusted my expectations from making it to the NBA to playing professional basketball anywhere, which would still be a major achievement.

I ended up playing for a team in Australia; then, the following year, for a team in Greece; and the year after that, for a different team in Spain. Three years of "professional" basketball may sound pretty cool, but it was a far cry from what most people would envision. If you've seen the movie *Semi-Pro*, then you've got an idea of what it was actually like. The players were more interested in the parties after the games than the game themselves.

After that third year, I got cut from the Spanish team. It was a pretty low point. I'd been all-in and had no backup plan. It felt like insult added to injury. My initial goal had been dashed, and now I'd lasted only three years as a professional, to the extent one could even call it that. At the age of twenty-four, I felt like a failure.

I returned to Kearney and moved back in with my parents, like an animal licking its wounds. I was feeling sorry for myself and perceiving myself as a failure. In my mind, all those who'd doubted me had been proven right. My mom, attempting to buoy me up, would put spins on standard inspirational quotes, my favorite of which was, "When one door closes, four open, plus an entire beachfront patio overlooking the ocean." It was hard not to be positive around her.

I realized then that all the energy I'd poured into wanting to play in the NBA was in fact setting me up for something different. What I could do best was coach and train others. While it wasn't my destiny to end up at the highest levels of basketball, I could help prepare and guide those whose physical gifts and mental desire did provide the right foundation. In that moment, my goal changed. I said, "I'm going to coach in the NBA."

I was back at square one. I had no credentials and no connections. If people had been skeptical about my goal of playing Division I, they now more or less laughed in my face. They asked when I was going to just settle down and get a normal, stable job. In the Midwest, by the time you're in your mid-twenties, you're expected to be married and have a standard nine-to-five desk gig.

I wasn't going to accept being like everyone else. I kicked into an even higher gear, cold-calling and writing letters to every general manager in the NBA, not explicitly asking for a job but demonstrating my knowledge, expressing my passion, and sharing my thoughts. I tailored each letter, and at the end of each said I'd welcome the chance to play any type of role.

Out of all these contacts, I received a single response – from Gary Sacks, general manager of the Los Angeles Clippers at the time. He told me if I were ever out in L.A., I could look him up. The same day, I took all my savings, asked my parents for a loan, and bought a plane ticket for the following week, letting Gary know I'd be in town. I told him I was heading there to run a basketball camp, since I didn't want to seem like a stalker.

I prepared like crazy for the meeting, knowing it might be my only shot. Gary kept his word, arranging to meet for coffee. The conversation was great; I felt we hit it off, and hoped he felt the same, though I wasn't sure.

Of course, I knew Gary wasn't going to just put me in the NBA. I had to make them want me. My only real skill was shooting. So I created a customized basketball design, featuring a line down the middle, and found a place in China to manufacture it for me. I had to take another loan from my parents. The balls could only be delivered to a place in Oakland, so, once they were ready, I drove the twenty-nine hours there from Kansas City to pick them up. Then I spent the next five years marketing myself like crazy, traveling everywhere I could, and running camps for anyone who would let me. Eventually I found a sweet spot doing camps for international schools, since they spoke English, had money, and loved basketball.

At one point, I found myself running a camp for a youth basketball league in Melbourne. One morning, I woke up to see an email with the subject line, "Brooklyn Nets shooting coach." In the body of the email was a line offering me that position. I assumed it was spam and was about to delete it when a voice in my head told me to stop and keep reading. *We need a shooting coach, and we've heard you're the best.* The referral had come from a group of coaches I'd met at a Nike-run shooting camp in Asia, which I'd been recommended for because of my relationship with Gary Sacks. Many of the guys I'd worked with at that camp had gone on to become coaches in the NBA.

The next week, I was in Brooklyn, somehow having become their new shooting coach. That year, the team went from twenty-eighth in the league in three-point shooting to second. Things seemed to be on an upward trend. I was receiving a lot of publicity, being touted as the new kid with the bright future...and then a new coach was hired, who cleaned house, getting rid of lots of people, including me.

I was used to bumps in the road by now. I refused to let it deter me. You can't think of these moments as doors closing, but instead as pivots. The unknown is scary, but it's also exciting. Every effort you make in life is preparing you for multiple possibilities. Every part of yourself that you pour into one opportunity is also setting you up for another. I moved to Los Angeles, where Gary and his family generously allowed me to bunk in their guest room. He and I would become professional associates as well as true friends. I continued to work my network, offering my assistance and expertise to other teams and players. I started training some of them in the offseason. Other coaches in my circle brought me in to consult. I met lots of agents who connected me with the players they represented.

During that period, I developed a proprietary approach called The Breakthrough Formula, which consists of four key elements: confidence, cooperation, service and purpose. This formula now serves as the basis for my training program, and provided the material for a book I recently published. I realize now that my dream all along took the form of helping others realize their full potential in the sport I love. The first conception of your dream isn't necessarily the one you'll end up at. Our visions are meant to be adaptable. What I thought was intended to be a vision of me scoring baskets was in fact one of me helping others do so. Now I live that passion, not only helping change NBA players' lives but applying the principles of my formula to the broader game of life. In doing so, I've achieved greater success than I ever imagined, by helping others in a way I never realized I could.

Chapter 18: Appreciate the Power of Clarity

In past chapters, we've talked about defining your goals, making plans to meet them, implementing the steps to get there, and adjusting to the inevitable twists and turns that will arise along the way. Now let's talk about what those goals look like.

On the way toward your apex – your best, most effective, most successful you – you will pursue and achieve a series of individual goals. Think about a certain one right now. Can you picture yourself meeting it? Do you know what vision represents this accomplishment? Is the vision clear or fuzzy?

The clearer your picture of what you want to achieve, the better your chance of doing so. A lucid, consistent, coherent vision shows you what to focus on. It reminds you what you want to make real. It gives you a mental image to hold onto anytime you feel your energy or confidence waning. Think of the difference between a weak flashlight beam versus a powerful one, a washed-out photo taken in poor lighting versus one taken in ideal conditions with professional equipment, or driving in fog as opposed to clear conditions. The latter scenarios all provide superior clarity and vision – making it easier to find what you're looking for, see what you need to, or reach your intended destination. The vision of your apex may seem far away at first. Stay focused on it as you climb and watch it become clearer and clearer, until it's finally within your grasp.

Establishing a Vision

You have an idea. A notion. A concept. You know there's something there, you feel it, a kernel, a bud, a not-quite-yet-clear something that needs definition, like a blurry image you're downloading that hasn't yet come into focus. There's a kind of end state you're starting to vaguely imagine, a picture you know represents something significant, something that matters. It hasn't yet materialized – though it will.

Some visions arrive fully formed; others need time to crystallize. Often, the vision representing that important something will pop into vivid, exciting dimension when you least expect it – while taking a shower, singing in the car, walking out of the coffee shop, pushing your child in the stroller. Can you force a vision into fruition? No. However, you can certainly encourage it.

One way to do this is to make sure you really understand what a vision is, complementary to the other aspects of your apex pursuit such as mission or values. Mission is why you're doing what you're doing. Values are the principles that guide your decisions. Vision is just what it sounds like: the picture you want to achieve that represents the meeting of a goal.

What's your picture? The clearer and more precise it is, the better chance you have of meeting it. So force yourself to answer the key questions surrounding all three of these related aspects. Why do you want to pursue this goal? What are the values you'll adhere to as you engage in the pursuit? And what does the final vision of success look like? Maybe it's you holding a diploma. Maybe it's the startup you and two partners have just founded becoming public on the New York Stock Exchange. Maybe it's having made a measurable difference in the cleanliness of the oceans, the health of the rhino population, or the reduction of greenhouse emissions.

Another way to help develop a vision around a given goal is to actively experiment with different possibilities of what it could be. In business, this is sometimes called ideating (throwing all possibilities on the table), then iterating (developing an idea in steps).

Many renowned artists are known for having done painstaking experimentation with their own visions before beginning the actual work. Numerous cherished paintings have, through forensic analysis, revealed pencil sketches underneath. Countless pieces of great architecture began with elaborate blueprints that then became tiny scale models. Treasured books commonly started with the authors creating detailed character outlines and treatments dozens of pages long. Leonardo Da Vinci, among the most accomplished visionaries in history, famously left behind thousands of pages of notebooks containing an almost unthinkable array of ideas in various states of clarity, including, at least conceptually, the helicopter, the parachute, the calculator, the double hull, plate tectonics, and the use of solar power. Leonardo's lesson is a powerful one. Don't just wait for vision to strike. Work it.

Finally, there's a tool I like for facilitating the vision of a goal which I call the Question Ladder. It's a technique that involves gaining an awareness of the types of questions we ask ourselves, from the weakest questions to the strongest.

Let me explain what I mean by "weak" and "strong" questions. Certain types of inquiries we make tend to be negative, judgmental, condescending, or antagonistic in nature. These kinds of questions exist on the first rung of the ladder, and often begin with the word why. *Why did you do that when I asked you not to? Why did you marry him when all of us could see it was a mistake? Why did you make that choice if it was so risky?* Often, these first-rung questions only highlight a failure or mistake. Consequently, they just as often cause the person being asked to respond in a defensive and adversarial way.

On the second rung of the ladder are the types of questions that typically start with the word how, and aren't much more useful than those that begin with why. While these aren't interrogations like those on the first rung, they are, frequently, questions concerned with mere survival. *How do I turn this thing on? How do I get this damn copier to work? How do I cook spaghetti so that it isn't too hard or too soft?* We ask these questions when treading water in hope that the answers will get us past the current moment to the next.

The majority of the time, it is these first- and second-rung questions people ask themselves, even if they aren't the kinds of questions that push you toward your apex. To keep climbing, you need to ask yourself the questions that belong to the higher rungs, the inquiries that propel you forward, and upward.

On the third, fourth and fifth rungs, we begin to see questions that represent a growth mindset – questions that include words like when, where and what. *When will that course be available? Where do I need to go for that important meeting? What is the next level I can get to?* And at the top rung are questions containing the most influential word of all: who. *Who can tell me more about this subject? Who would be the best person to ask for help with this task? Who do I wish to become?*

I characterize the typical questions on the first rung as *failing*, those on the second as *surviving*, those on the third, fourth and fifth as *thriving*, and those on the sixth, or top, rung, as *succeeding*. Apex achievers ask lots of questions all the time, and the ones they ask most often are the ones belonging to the top rungs of the ladder – the ones that help build a clear vision, making it easier to pursue the goal that vision represents.

Refining an Existing Vision

The vision in your mind may be almost there, yet not quite. It needs something to help it take shape. Those who wear glasses or contact lenses do so to enhance their vision and bring things into clearer focus. The visions representing your goals warrant the same attention and potential upgrading. Just as prescriptions change over time, these images should be subject to the same potential fine-tuning.

Always trust your vision, even if it runs counter to what's come before. Believe in what you see, even if no one else does, or can. Maybe, even though they'd like to see it, too, they're more comfortable with the known and the easily observable. Maybe they take comfort in seeing what the majority of others do. Maybe the new vision is so grand and seemingly outlandish that, even though they believe you believe it, they themselves can't get there.

When, in the early seventeenth century, Galileo used his newfangled telescope to discover truths that undermined the traditional vision of an unchanging cosmos with Earth at the center, the Church freaked out, forcing him to recant under threat of torture. Sure, it eventually came around, admitting he was right a few centuries later. The moral, though, is clear. We can get overly comfortable with the visions suggested to us, and overly confident in the ideas that inform them. It can be easier to continue with what we already know than to consider something in a new light. However, visions can be both consistent and fluid.

In fact, the question ladder described above is one of my own examples of vision adjustment. When I first heard of this tool, it was referred to as the Question Pyramid. After a few years of teaching it this way, I thought about it further, received valuable feedback from others, and decided the ladder was a more appropriate metaphor for what I wanted it to communicate. Don't be afraid of altering your vision. We change, and the things around us change. So the way a certain goal looks may change over time, too.

Replacing a Vision

You might have seen a certain goal in one way, and now that vision doesn't work anymore, for any number of reasons. The industry is different. Ethics are different. Customer priorities are different. Technology is different. You're different. Life is different.

Even visions known for being clear, consistent and reliable sometimes need new articulation in response to an unexpected event, a shift in the sands, or a jolt from the competition.

In the early 2000s, the English luxury fashion house Burberry, despite its hundred-fifty-year heritage, suffered a hooligan hijacking and had to refine its image urgently. Famous for distinct red-and-beige checked patterns and trench raincoats, the company had, through no intention of its own, become synonymous with gang wear throughout the UK when bands of delinquents all over the region started adopting the style. Things got so bad, and the brand so associated with thuggery, that English pubs started banning anyone wearing its items from entering their premises. Taking decisive action, the company revamped its classic look and staple pieces, transforming the image with the help of elegant celebrity endorsers. The successful reimaging cleverly shifted the company's brand from hooligan to hot and in fact resulted in higher sales than ever and expansion into new global markets.

In 2004, shock filmmaker Morgan Spurlock made the documentary *Super Size Me*, casting McDonald's in a terrible light. Following the release of the film, in which Spurlock existed entirely on McDonald's fare for a month to see what it would do to him, the chain had to think fast given the extremely bad publicity with which it was getting bombarded for promoting unhealthy eating and contributing to increasing obesity. Seemingly overnight, healthier options such as salads and wraps appeared on the menu, as well as the opening of McCafé concessions offering premium coffees and herbal teas, and the negative talk was soon forgotten. Moving the focus from health crisis to health-conscious allowed the chain to maintain what had made it so successful in the first place – everyone still loves a McDonald's burger and fries – while expanding its vision and winning new customers as a result.

In 2010, Old Spice had been around for seventy-five years, however it was quickly becoming known as a stodgy old brand – your grandfather's deodorant – and losing market share to competitors whose images were edgier or seen as more hip. Enlisting an attractive former NFL player as its new spokesman, the company designed a cheeky new campaign touting the virtues of masculinity, launched it during Super Bowl weekend, focused on its new line of body wash soaps, and expertly leveraged social media to connect with younger consumers, creating an interactive viral sensation. Old Spice became brand new, overhauling its image and propelling itself to the very top of the mountain, its body washes eventually outselling all others. Like Burberry and McDonald's, the company had stayed true to its fundamental self while properly recognizing the need to update its vision.

In Chapter Eleven, I talked about the low point I was at in late 2005 while living in Las Vegas, and the multiple destructive habits I was engaged in. This included starting a damaging relationship with someone who treated me poorly, which I was accepting since my own self-worth was so low. A few months after I'd entered into the relationship, the two of us traveled to Los Angeles for the wedding of one of my closest friends and a reunion with my other closest ones. This was the handful of guys who had played a large part in changing the direction of my life in high school after my dad had told me in no uncertain terms that most of the people I was hanging around with were not exactly contributing to me becoming my best self.

It didn't take my friends long to see the toxic nature of the relationship. After an evening that included an incident of abuse from the person I was with, my friends staged a spontaneous intervention, confronting me about the relationship, telling me I was worth more than that, and urging me to find someone who would treat me the way I deserved to be treated.

By carrying out this loving ambush, my friends caused me to re-evaluate both the relationship I'd allowed myself into and what it represented in terms of the trajectory of my life. They made me see that I needed to replace my vision of myself, my own value, and what I could become.

Soon after, I found a job opportunity in Washington State. When I flew there to be interviewed, I came into the office in the morning and met a woman who made an immediate, and powerful, impression on me in a way I couldn't quite describe.

I did a partial move as fast as possible, leaving some of my stuff in storage in Las Vegas. When I traveled back there, I realized I didn't have enough money for a moving service. My former boss generously offered to fund the move, on one condition: I had to create a Missing Person's Report and show it to her. Thinking I must have misheard, I asked her to repeat what she'd said. "You heard me," she replied. "I'll need you to fill out a Missing Person's Report."

She explained the tool she was referring to: a detailed description of a figure who was missing from one's life. What she was asking of me was to write down, in as much detail as possible, the characteristics of a person I would like to have in my life who was not currently in it.

That evening, I started listing things. Non-smoker. No kids. Spur-of-the-moment singer. Redhead. Attractive curves. It went on. And felt odd, describing in such detail this figment who would need to satisfy so narrow a profile. I gave my boss the report, accepted her kind offer to pay, and shipped my things.

What I came to discover not long after was that the person I'd met on that first day, whose name I'd learned was Nita, checked a few of the boxes on the list I'd made. That was from our initial few conversations. The more we interacted, the more I was astounded to find that she matched nearly the entire list. My boss, not unlike my friends had done, forced me into greater clarity, along with the forward movement and easier decision-making that accompanies it.

One day, Nita asked me if I'd like to get a drink after work. (Yes – she asked me! Thank god she had more courage than I did.) We went to a wine bar nearby. I was attempting to contain my excitement as much as possible, hoping she was feeling the same spark. At one point, she excused herself, went to make a call, and returned, grinning. She would later divulge to me that the call she'd made was to cancel a date that she had for later that evening.

A few hours later, after we'd walked around town and gone dancing at a club (since we were both too nervous to eat dinner), it was time to say goodnight, which for me meant going back to the basement of the friend who was letting me stay at his place until I could find one of my own. We said goodnight, and, senses swimming, I got in my car, which still had Vegas plates. Soon after, I saw flashing lights in my rear-view. After I pulled over, the cop made me go through a series of sobriety tests: following his finger with my eyes (I moved my whole head without knowing it), walking heel-to-toe seven steps in one direction and then the other (I took two steps and stumbled), and lifting one leg followed by the other and counting to ten (I lifted one leg and got to four before falling over). He pulled out a breathalyzer and asked me to blow into it. I didn't quite grasp the gravity of the situation because I was so in the clouds. After I'd complied, the officer looked at the readout, then back at me, and said, "If I didn't see this for myself, I wouldn't have believed it. The reading is zero. You just suck at field sobriety tests."

"I don't think so," I said with a smile. I asked him if I could get back in my car. No, he said – my license was suspended in Nevada and I had fifteen minutes to get my car off the road. I called Nita back, and she came. We parked my car in the Dairy Queen across the street (without getting to enjoy an ice cream since it was now one o'clock a.m.) before she drove me back to my friend's. It was the best two first dates in one night ever. I'd never seen more clearly.

Shawna's Story

I came from a corporate background in which it was expected that you worked hard and showed up. Valued above all else were face time at the office and hours on the clock. Things like taking vacation were not. Indulging in such personal luxuries was in fact frowned upon, as though doing so was a sign of lacking dedication. As a single mom focused on paying the bills and providing for my son, I did what was expected.

When I started doing sessions with a coach, one of the things he asked me was what goals I had. I said my goal was to take care of my son. Yes, he said, and what about my goals? What did I want to achieve for me? I said it wasn't really something I thought about. He asked me how and when I celebrate myself or my accomplishments. I told him I don't.

He pushed me to start visualizing specific, tangible goals that were about me – goals I aimed to achieve, rewards I hoped to realize. He wouldn't accept vague answers or fuzzy pictures, which I appreciated. Still, I instinctively resisted at first, unaccustomed as I was to thinking about such things, much less putting them in real terms.

Another thing he asked me was to name a place I'd always wanted to go. I told him I had no idea. Seriously, he said, where's somewhere you've always wanted to visit. I heard myself say, "A beach with clear water." Then I heard myself add, "I'd like to walk in the water and run my fingers along the surface." It was an almost reflexive response. I grew up in Connecticut. The beaches there were characterized by dirty water and lots of rocks, and for a long time, I thought that's what beaches looked like everywhere. Then I grew up, saw pictures of other beaches, and realized just how wrong I was.

The coach asked me to name a specific place, somewhere with those dream beaches. I said, how am I supposed to know? He told me, what if you suddenly had the chance to go, today, if you had that opportunity, where would that place be? So I Googled places with white sand and clear water and came up with a random answer: Antigua.

I want you to start putting the trip together, he said. What do you mean? I asked. He told me he wanted me to investigate all the details, including costs, logistics – everything short of actually booking it. When we speak next, he said, you're going to describe the trip to me.

This was difficult for me to do, because, again, I had long put my own dreams on hold. It was a mentality that had been reinforced by others, who told me that's just how it is, and it's just what you do. The coach pushing me to visualize helped me embrace the value of setting my own goals and associated rewards. What also helped was moving to a different company with a culture in which hard work was appreciated, as was taking care of oneself.

The final piece of the puzzle was being pushed to envision both the goal itself along with the steps needed to achieve it. I was struggling financially, and just couldn't see how this would be feasible. Nonetheless, I did the research, found a beautiful resort – not to mention learning where Antigua was, which I didn't know when I'd named it – and put together a budget to share with my coach. He asked me to put the trip cost in actionable terms: What would it take for me to afford this trip, and by when? I calculated that I'd need to increase my output by about twenty percent within the next year. Suddenly it seemed more realistic. I can do that, I said. He replied, "Good, now we know everything about this trip except one: When are you taking it?"

I said I wanted to go a year from then. A few unforeseen obstacles – some health issues, a car accident – delayed my intended timeline. Ultimately, that wasn't important. What mattered was the shift in mentality I'd undergone after setting a vision for myself. My performance and results ticked up right away, and over the subsequent months, continued to grow. I positioned myself for the trip in practical terms. Just as important, I came to feel that I deserved it, and that doing so didn't mean taking away from others. Even my son told me I needed to do more for myself. I didn't even own a passport before. I went and got one.

I still sometimes battle with my own sense of value, and therefore with my right to do things for me. The old Shawna is still there, along with her self-doubt and lack of personal entitlement. The new Shawna's voice gets stronger every day, and the old Shawna's a bit easier to ignore. With my new mindset and appreciation for the power of clarity, I know I can accomplish whatever I want to. I've placed a picture of that beach in Antigua on my vision board, and there it will stay until the moment I step on the plane.

Chapter 19: Wear Your Trophies Proudly

In previous chapters, we've covered a lot of ground regarding the kinds of plans to make, the kinds of steps to take, and the overall approaches and practical strategies that can provide structure, organization, direction and clarity to maximize the odds of success in whatever endeavor you pursue.

Along this journey, there are going to be blips and bumps. No one's life is a straight line; everyone's is a messy finger painting, and all the more exciting because of it. As you walk along the path, you splash through different puddles that throw onto the canvas of your life endless colors, in untold patterns. The painting of your existence becomes ever richer, evolving in texture and shifting in tone with each new step.

Each of these pieces of color and pattern represents a different experience that contributes to the unique person you are, and each one, for that reason, has its own value. Some of these experiences last a moment, some a month; some represent triumph, others tribulation; certain ones stay vivid in your memory forever, others fade with time.

There are the external, those marked by physical evidence of our experience: the sprained ankle from playing basketball, the scar from your C-section, the photo of you at the swimming hole with your friends, poised to wrap your feet around the rope and launch. And the internal, the moments symbolized by their emotional impact: the particular smell of grass that forever calls to mind your childhood day camp, the dream you have every year or so about walking into the exam only to realize you haven't studied, the song that nearly makes you pull over every time you hear it because of that certain person it always makes you think of.

These are the events and occurrences that make up your life, the individual bits and pieces that form the mosaic of you as a person. As you pursue your apex, every one of these highs and lows, victories and defeats, successes and stumbles are there to remind you who you are, why you are, and that you're meant to be this exactly, with all the power and potential to accomplish anything you desire.

All Your Experiences Are Rewards

We tend to describe our experiences according to labels of good and bad, or at least to assign them a place along a positive-negative spectrum.

The plaque you won for being salesperson of the month is positive; the Most Improved crest from seventh grade, somewhat positive; the dent you put in your dad's rear fender, definitely not positive.

Change that perspective. Understand that each of these is a building block that adds to your cumulative ability – to win, to lose, to nail it, to slip up, to learn, to cope, to rebound, to persist, to succeed. Every experience you have means you assimilate a piece of something new into who and what you are. The difference between that plaque, the crest and the dent is nothing. Thinking of the first as a mark of achievement, the second as a half-embarrassing nod and the third as a mistake with potentially frightening consequences is false.

What these all have in common is that they are pieces of testimony to your development as a person, with your own discrete mix of experiences that no one else in the world has. As the Nike poster on my teenage friend's wall said, *Life is not a spectator sport.* Every acknowledgement of your participation in it, whether medal, crest or dent, offers you something worthwhile.

It's important to separate the feelings we have in response to a given experience from the value of the experience itself. Yes, it's fair to say you had a good feeling when handed the plaque, that you felt conflicted accepting the Most Improved award, and that you were scared to death after backing your dad's car into the post. These are emotions associated with the experiences. They don't characterize the experience itself as positive or negative. Our involvement in our own lives is more complex and nuanced than that. Perhaps you won the monthly sales award yet fell short of your own personal goal, which you then exceeded the next month, even though that month you didn't win the award. Suppose you didn't just get the Most Improved crest – the improvement was so dramatic that you also won the English and Math awards. Maybe, after you confessed to your dad about the car, the experience became indelible mostly for the way he told you everyone makes mistakes and said he was proud of you for admitting it.

Even – or maybe especially – the experiences that, in the moment we have them, we may wish we didn't. If you think about the slightly morbid expression, "What doesn't kill you makes you stronger," well, that means every single experience in your life makes you stronger except the very last one. That's a lot of growth!

Or maybe you prefer the way it was put by the nineteenth-century theologian John Henry Newman: "Growth is the only evidence of life." That growth may take the form of "getting stronger," and can also be defined by acquiring knowledge, gaining wisdom, earning insight, finding your passion, stumbling upon your superpower, or noticing blind spots. None of these things is inherently positive or negative – they simply represent your broadening over time.

"Life is the art of drawing without an eraser," said John William Gardner, and he was right. You build a beautiful, wild, unpredictable mural as you go, each part of it under the title, Your Life. Certain psychological studies suggest we don't reach full maturity until, on average, age sixty (which explains why I like the same jokes ten-year-olds do). What a nice long time to watch your mural only begin to take shape.

Embracing Experience

There is an ongoing debate among parents today about whether kids get rewarded too easily for too little, the most frequent example being trophies given for participation as opposed to winning, or at least excelling. Parents worry their kids will grow up to be lazy, entitled slackers because they received undeserved accolades for a given experience.

The parents shouldn't worry. We grow through the responses we have to our experiences, which are almost always honest and accurate, and the reflections on those responses. A ten-year-old understands as much as a thirty-year-old does how connected a material piece of evidence is to the effort he put into something. You don't need your parents or anyone else to interpret a trophy or any other mark of experience. The truth of what it represents is what it means to you. What matters most is to wrap your arms around every one of those experiences and embrace the lessons they can teach and the growth they can inspire.

Be proud to be able to say, "I made this mistake, and here's what I learned from it." Give yourself credit when you can point to a previous version of yourself and know what you did to strive for better. Practice going beyond how an experience felt to understanding what it meant. Take time to sink down deep into these reflections and come back up an enhanced you, more self-aware and self-assured.

Komodo dragons, those unique apex animals who can grow up to ten feet long and three hundred pounds, have bony, variously patterned deposits within their skin, under the armored scales protecting it, called osteoderms. Here's the cool thing: these giant lizards aren't born with their distinct markings. Just as rings reveal the approximate age of a tree, osteoderms provide evidence of a Komodo dragon's life: they develop with age, becoming more extensive and variable over time, and telling, at least partially, the vigorous stories of competition, protection and survival undertaken even by these creatures who sit atop their environment, over spans that can last up to thirty years.

In this way, we're similar to trees, Komodo dragons, and every other living creature. We collect the marks of our experience as we go, developing layers and acquiring evidence, some in the material form of trophies and plaques, some in the intangible form of emotions and reflections. Every experience in your life bears witness to who you have been, are now, and have the potential to become. Together, they are badges to show you what you've both accomplished and endured. They are marks of achievement and scars of battle. They remind you that you're here, an active participant in life, changing all the time, evolving constantly, continuing to climb.

Lilly's Story

You can't decide which cards you're dealt or the circumstances you're born into. What you can decide is the way you live your life. I remind myself of this every day and use it as my guiding principle. It helps me embrace my life as a whole, including the highs and lows, the good moments and bad. All of them contribute to who I've become today.

My mom had me when she was still a teenager. During the first nine years of my life, I was shuttled through the foster system and moved around from one family member to another. These weren't people who knew me or cared about me. They were just relatives who were willing to take me in until they weren't. In the summers, my mom would send me to stay with my grandfather, who sexually abused me from the time I was six until I was fourteen. When I told my mom about it, she refused to believe me. It was probably easier for her that way.

When I turned nine, my mom took me back in – mostly because she'd had another daughter by a different man and needed a babysitter. Those were pretty bad years. I'd go from taking care of my half-sister to absorbing my mom's constant physical and verbal abuse to tuning her out as best I could when she'd tell me over and over that I wouldn't graduate high school, or that I was going to fall prey to drugs, or that I was sure to end up pregnant.

My instinctive response was to become her opposite. She was a miserable person, she was always angry, she went from guy to guy, marriage to marriage. I chose to be different – starting with adopting and maintaining a positive attitude no matter what. I vowed I would always treat others well. I took care of myself, becoming independent much earlier than a young person normally would. From age thirteen, I worked two jobs. In high school, I paid for my own books, my clothes, everything. Despite my mom's cruel predictions, I did graduate, and, immediately afterwards, enrolled in the military so I could get away. I had the honor of serving my country for six years.

As I matured, due to a combination of faith, therapy and the benefit of adult perspective, I came to forgive my mom and the way she'd been toward me. I realized that she herself was still a kid when she had me. My father had taken off. She hadn't a clue how to parent. She'd come from a very large family and had grown up in a household where the example she saw every day was a mom who'd treated her horrendously. So she had no positive role model, no partner, and no idea how to raise a child. She did the best she could. No, it wasn't good. It was simply what she'd been given to work with. Today, after a lot of hard work and tough conversations, we've managed to develop a pretty good relationship. It feels gratifying, and also liberating.

The other big trauma in my life was my first husband's suicide. I'd met him after leaving the military. We were together about twelve years, married for nine. We both had jobs, we'd just gone on vacation, everything felt normal. After seeing a movie one evening, I told him I was going out to the drugstore. When I got back, I found him hanging from our basketball hoop. His taking his own life was a shock to me and everyone else who knew him. I hadn't seen any signs. He left no note. I'll never know what demons were haunting him.

168

I sold my house and moved across the country, where my sister and her family lived. Among many other difficult emotions, for a long time I carried intense survivor guilt. I wanted to join him, ask what drove him to such a thing, understand what I could or should have done differently. Three years of counseling and therapy, along with lots of support from friends, helped me start to process all my feelings one small step at a time and slowly move forward. Move back into living life.

I took his ashes to a place he loved. When I arrived, a dog appeared and started following me around. It stayed with me all the way to the outdoor chapel, and to the site where I spread the ashes. Sometime after, I looked up to see that the dog was no longer there. There had been a moment a few years before when we'd been watching a movie about a man who dies and then returns to life in the form of a dog, and my husband had casually said, "If I go, and then you see a dog, don't worry. It's just me." I keep this to myself, to smile at and wonder about privately.

We all experience challenges and traumas over the course of a lifetime. Sharing them isn't for the sake of soliciting sympathy or pity. It's to help yourself own those experiences so you can work through them and continue moving along the journey. When I tell others about these moments that have tested me, they often ask how I got through them. My answer is simple: I didn't have a choice. You can either go forward or remain in place. Life is going to throw things at you. You can't predict what they are or how hard they're going to be. Making the decision to enjoy life despite these challenges is freeing. I force myself to live every day, throw myself into my existence, and focus on life's joys and gifts. The scars are inevitable. It's up to you how you wear them.

Chapter 20: Set Clear Finish Lines

In the previous chapters, we've talked about many factors that contribute to achieving your apex. Knowing where you want to go in order to guarantee you get there. Defining your goals in clear terms in order to hold yourself accountable. Charting a logical path in order to make sure you keep moving forward. Now, let's talk about that finish line you're aiming for.

Some goals are naturally self-contained, like finishing a course or degree. Others lend themselves to continuation or upgrading, such as mastering a certain weight at the bench press or deadlift until it becomes comfortable and you increase the task by upping the load, adding reps, increasing range of motion, or decreasing rest. Whether your current goal stands in isolation or is meant to lead elsewhere, the most important thing is that, while it's the goal, it's the goal, fixed and defined, set in its place, ready for you to meet it.

Mirages, Scope Creep and a Round Earth

Think about when you're driving on a hot summer day and you see the illusion of rippling oil near the surface of the road. The reasons behind this perceptual trick are the same ones that cause people wandering in the desert to think they see water when they don't. It's a simple matter of the hot asphalt or sand interacting with the cooler air above it and distorting the light rays in a way that makes us uncertain of what's really up ahead.

In other words, when the factors influencing our goals aren't aligned or consistent, they mess with our ability to see clearly, to move ahead confidently, and to remain on course. Since Chapter One, we've talked about optimizing your chances for success by doing things like creating positive conditions, identifying your strengths, defining goals, making plans, anticipating obstacles, and being willing to give and get help. Now that you've put it all together, promise yourself you'll keep that goal where you've set it.

You may have heard the term "scope creep" as it pertains to business. At the start of any project, it's important to establish what the intended work aims to accomplish, using which resources, according to what timeline, and within what boundaries. This is commonly agreed to without much fuss, since those involved are generally unified in answering these questions at the outset.

It's when something threatens to alter the parameters that things get hairy. An outside consultant is brought in who suggests modifications to the initial goals. The leader of the core project team changes roles, and their replacement feels the project should have a broader set of outcomes. Other divisions get wind of the initiative and ask to become involved.

Any of these possibilities, and many others, can change the nature or position of the finish line if you allow them to. Once you do, a slippery slope can take hold, and before you know it, the objectives you originally defined look different. Maybe a little different, maybe a lot. Regardless, when you permit scope creep – allowing the boundaries of your goal to change – the more difficult your task becomes, and the more complicated it is to meet. When our intended destination shifts, the likelihood of reaching it changes, and the way it fits into our overall plans can be affected. Though the path toward achieving your apex doesn't have to be linear – it hardly ever is – the end point itself shouldn't be allowed to wander.

Unless there's a good reason for it. Early ancient peoples believed the Earth was flat. To their perception, that meant if you sailed too far in any direction, you'd eventually fall off the edge. Then the Phoenicians, while traveling around Africa, found that the sun was no longer directly above them and had instead moved to their right, which couldn't be the case if the planet were flat. Later, Aristotle noticed that when ships reached the horizon, rather than vanishing over the imagined edge, they would disappear slowly from the bottom up, which could only be the case if Earth was a sphere. Later still, astronomers saw from the shadow cast by the Earth on the moon that our big blue marble is most certainly a globe, and not a disc.

While it seems silly to us today that the same people who came up with written language, the calendar, the plow, door locks and toothpaste could also believe in a flat Earth, we need to remember that they held this collective belief based on the general evidence around them and the views of the majority. It took the conviction and clarity of specific individuals to shift the shared understanding. To us in the modern world, it's common knowledge that you can walk toward the horizon forever and it will remain (apart from a select few "flat-Earthers" who…never mind, don't get me

171

started). It made sense for this idea to overturn the earlier one. Be willing to adjust your horizons when there are good reasons for doing so. Never do so at the whims of others or to align with the most common view. Your goals are yours, you know why you've set them, and if they are to be altered, only you should be allowed to alter them.

Reaching Your Goals, Then Reaching Beyond

Whether or not your goals warrant adjustment along the way, once they're set, go after them with everything you've got while resisting looking farther ahead. Don't look past your immediate destination while pursuing it; target a new one after you get there.

The football term "moving the chains" is a great analogy for this principle. Though the execution of the sport is complex, its rules for scoring points are simple. The field is one hundred yards long. The team with the ball has four consecutive plays in which to gain ten yards. If they achieve this task, they are awarded another four plays to attempt to gain another ten yards. This continues until they either reach the other team's end zone and earn points or fail to gain the ten yards and hand over possession.

On the sidelines, two individuals hold vertical orange flags exactly ten yards apart connected by a chain along the ground. Throughout the game, this pair moves anytime the team does, so that there is always a clear indication of where it is starting on a given play and where it must reach in order to keep going. When a team gains the precious ten yards that allows them to proceed, it is referred to as "moving the chains." Meet one goal, then look to the next.

This simple yet profound lesson, at least in the realm of weight training, is said to have been handed down to us by a man named Milo of Croton, who lived in the 6th century BC in a Greek colony of southern Italy. A six-time Olympic champion and the most renowned wrestler of antiquity, Milo embodied the most fundamental principle of strength training, called progressive overload. Legend has it that, as a young man, he began carrying a calf every day from its birth until it became a full-sized ox. As the animal grew, so did Milo's strength. (It's also said that he carried an ox on his shoulders into the Olympic stadium. Talk about playing head games with your opponents.)

The principle communicated to us by this ancient Olympian is elegant in its simplicity: a muscle needs to experience increasing challenges to become stronger. Or, once you've conquered one threshold, aim for a new one, by applying the lessons we've discussed throughout the book: forcing yourself out of your comfort zone; designing and following a plan; being precise and focused in your execution; allowing yourself strategic periods of rest and recovery; and remembering that we all get knocked off the horse sometimes, and what matters is how you get back on.

Important peaks aren't reached in one shot. They require time, focus, patience and adjustments along the way. When people attempt to climb Mount Everest, do they just look up from the bottom, grab a bottle of water, and go? Hardly. They must follow a precise plan designed to take them from one step to another, until finally – hopefully – reaching the summit. This is serious business. As with any meaningful apex, there is a clear start and end, which include a series of sub-goals that must be achieved along the way, in order.

Why, for example, must climbers spend time at base camp before striking out for the long ascent? What's the big deal? If someone is in reasonable shape, couldn't they just take a deep breath and, you know, go for it?

Certainly not. In fact, just getting to base camp involves a major effort. Aspiring climbers usually fly into Kathmandu in Nepal, then to the smaller Lukla Airport. From there, they trek upward, along the valley of the Dudh Kosi River to the Sherpa capital of Namche Bazaar, which sits at a little over eleven thousand feet. This journey takes about two days. There, they typically rest for about a day to get acclimatized to the altitude. They then trek for another two days to the village of Dingboche, which is at nearly fourteen thousand feet, before resting another day to acclimatize further. After another two days of travel, they reach base camp via the small uninhabited settlement of Gorakshep (if climbing from the south side), at an altitude of just above eighteen thousand feet.

So, yeah, "base" camp is a bit of a misnomer. (For contrast, my home of Birch Bay, Washington, sits at a rather comfortable ten feet above sea level.) Climbers then remain for several days to continue allowing their bodies to adjust to the fact that they have for some reason decided to see what it's like in the "death zone." (Or maybe the reason is frighteningly simple, as author Jon Krakauer puts it in his famous book *Into Thin Air*:

"Once Everest was determined to be the highest summit on Earth, it was only a matter of time before people decided that Everest needed to be climbed.")

Those who reach the mystical peak do so only through a carefully prescribed set of mini-finish lines, none of which can be reached ahead of any other. Attaining each individual milestone allows them to pursue the next, and, ultimately, to reach the pinnacle. They have succeeded in each individual achievement by giving it dedicated focus and maximum effort. You don't climb one section of a mountain while thinking about another. You focus on the goal you're pursuing. By keeping the next destination firm in your mind and clear in your vision, you make that goal more likely to hit, while at the same time preparing yourself for the next pursuit.

Indeed, challenging though these endeavors are, we all know the usual response of someone who has succeeded in conquering one mountain: seeking another to climb. As Krakauer correctly notes, that's our nature. And now that we've reached this destination, let me wish you every success in the journey toward your own apex.